Secrets & Lies in the United Kingdom:
Analysis of Political Corruption

SECRETS & LIES

IN THE UNITED KINGDOM

ANALYSIS OF POLITICAL CORRUPTION

FABIENNE PORTIER-LE COCQ, ed.

Westphalia Press
An Imprint of the Policy Studies Organization
Washington, DC
2017

Westphalia Press
An imprint of Policy Studies Organization
1527 New Hampshire Ave., NW
Washington, D.C. 20036
info@ipsonet.org

ISBN-10: 1-63391-593-X
ISBN-13: 978-1-63391-593-0

Cover and interior design by Jeffrey Barnes
jbarnesbook.design

Daniel Gutierrez-Sandoval, Executive Director
PSO and Westphalia Press

Updated material and comments on this edition
can be found at the Westphalia Press website:
www.westphaliapress.org

INTRODUCTION

Fabienne Portier-Le Cocq (ed.)
Université François Rabelais, Tours

It may appear paradoxical to address the topic of Secret and Lies at a time when digital technology enables people's private lives to be exposed to social networking sites either openly, forcibly, or out of personal choice. Internet users thus experience the loss of the notion of privacy, and the vulnerability of information with more or less porosity, whether it is voluntary or mastered; and hardly any secrets remain to be unveiled.

On the other hand, the Internet allows difficult-to-reach information to be accessed, if one thinks, for instance of terrorism. For security matters, hardly anyone would object to a lack of transparency and openness in that respect, on the basis of the public's right to know. The fact remains that the surveillance of home-grown groups (Aldrich 2005, 338), such as fringe groups, British group leaders, peace campaigners, and criminal rights activists, also provides a means to encroach upon liberties.

Findings based on a 4-year survey[1] carried out by Dr. Lawrence McNamara[2] suggest that accessing information about terrorism is difficult to get hold of, even legally.

> Everyone accepts that sometimes information must remain secret but it is crucial that we ensure that, whenever possible, what governments do in the name of their citizens is made visible and can be subjected to adequate scrutiny. Rights, security and accountability are all of the very highest importance; the way that governments and courts manage transparency is crucial in achieving all of them. (McNamara 2014)

---

1   From 2009 to 2013, Lawrence McNamara held an ESRC/AHRC Fellowship in Ideas and Beliefs under the Research Councils UK Global Uncertainties priority. This supported research which analyzed the relationships between democratic traditions of media freedom and the contemporary demands of national and international security (http://www.biicl.org/lawrencemcnamara).

2   Dr. Lawrence McNamara, Bingham Centre for the Rule of Law, London, helped shape the Justice and Security Act 2013.

For Michel Foucault (1979), truth is a way of exercising power, as power and knowledge are closely linked. Information is power, and, for states, citizens should not know everything about their nation. While for British contemporary writer Jonathan Coe "lying, for political and religious leaders, would rather be to tell half-truth" (COE 2015).[3]

The Official Secrets Act of 1911 stipulated that it was a criminal offence for a civil servant to disclose any unauthorized security and intelligence information (Aldrich 2005, 345). The act was replaced by the new Official Secrets Act in 1989 and served as a backdrop under Margaret Thatcher's governments in the prosecutions of Sarah Tisdall (1984) and Clive Ponting (1985), who had both leaked information. Richard Aldrich (2005, 333) contends that images of the secret state were schizophrenic, since popular spy fiction as depicted by film-makers and authors[4] and facts depicted in the press have for some time been poles apart.

The large-scale spate of revelations disclosed on an everyday basis in 2010 on WikiLeaks, the website created in 2006 by its founder, Australian-born journalist Julian Assange, disclosed documents from the U.S. State Department classified as "confidential" or "secret." It is considered to be one of the major leaks in military history. But WikiLeaks continues to work and unveil secrets. Although it is not a big group, it comprises people who preserve their anonymity to prevent themselves from being sued and use coded information to secure data. Encoding and ciphering are so strong that international intelligence agencies cannot crack their codes. Behind the Wikileaks case lies digital technology and its potential consequences, the infinite space that the Internet represents, state secrets, transparency versus opacity, and freedom of information.

In November 2015, the UK Government announced that Government Communications Headquarters (GCHQ), a British intelligence and security organization, and the National Crime Agency (NCA) would work together to tackle serious crimes and child pornography on the Dark Web. In late winter 2016, the British government launched a dedicated cybercrime unit to tackle the Dark Web. The Dark Web, part of the Deep Web, refers to dangerous secret online worlds. It hosts websites whose IP addresses of the

---

3   Impressions D'Europe. Jonathan Coe, *Rencontres littéraires anglaises (English Literature Festival)*, le Grand T, Nantes, November 28, 2015.

4   For instance, Ian Fleming's James Bond, an intelligence officer of the Secret Intelligence Service (SIS), referred to as M16.

servers, which run them, are hidden. Information is stolen by, and traded in, by hackers. For instance, cyber security experts endeavor to protect the details of credit cards up for sale on the Dark Web and sold for very little cost. It is notoriously known for hiding child pornography and for buying and selling drugs and weapons.

From a legal viewpoint, secrecy also applies when providing new identity and anonymity to protect witnesses or to free murderers. The infamous Jon Venables and Robert Thompson, who tortured and murdered 2-year-old James Bulger in 1993, saw their freedom preserved and personal details protected accordingly.

Most people no longer have a private life because they post it on social media, although some keep it secret. Family secrets make the headlines and the onset of DNA testing has made it possible to uncover personal or family secrets (Smart 2009, 551). In the United Kingdom, until the 1960s with respect to adoption, and the 1980s with respect to assisted reproduction, children were led to believe that their social parents were their biological ones (Smart 2009, 553). Moreover, prior to 1969, by law, a child born to a married woman was the legitimate child of her husband (Smart 2010, 398). John Eekelaar (2006) and Mhairi Cowden (2006; 2012) argue that it is every child's right to know his origins. Family secrets that are related to conception and reproduction are "a time bomb ticking away" (Lord Justice Ward 1996)[5].

According to Carol Smart (2009), The Mass Observation Archive (MOB) reveals that family secrets fall into four main arenas: (i) secrets pertaining to health, e.g. illnesses, disabilities, and mental disorders, (ii) secrecy about sexual orientation, i.e. homosexuality, (iii) finances and inheritance, and (iv) the broadest category of secrets touches on reproduction by disguising illegitimacy, adoption, premarital and medically assisted conceptions, and paternity. It is thus unsurprising that a recent cross-sectional qualitative study conducted in England[6] among 45 adults aged 20 to 85 has shown that the keywords principally associated with secrecy, secrets, and lies were the family, spouses, and children.

---

5   Lord Justice Ward, *Re H (A Minor) (Blood Tests: Parental Rights)*—[1996] 3 FCR 201 at 220, cited by C. Smart (2010), 397.

6   Fieldwork conducted by the author in two counties of the South East of England between 4th and 7th December 2015 and 9th and 11th January 2016.

The Royal Family of the United Kingdom is not exempt from secrecy. Prince John (1905–1919), the son of George V and Queen Mary and brother of the future King Edward VIII, suffered from epilepsy and was allegedly confined to a room in Sandringham (Bradford 2002; Channel 4 2008). On July 15, 2015, The Sun newspaper sparked a furore in Britain by releasing an archive footage from the 1930s of Queen Elizabeth II—then as a young girl—performing a Nazi salute in a home movie set at Balmoral castle in Scotland. The 17-second film showed the monarch, the Queen Mother at her side, Princess Margaret and their uncle, Prince Edward, Prince of Wales, who would later become King Edward VIII and abdicate in 1936. Dr. Karina Urbach of the Institute of Historical Research in London has described the footage as an "important historical document that asks serious questions of the Royal Family." The Sun explained its motive for publishing the film by stating the right for the public to finally see "the involvement of the Queens uncle Edward. These images have remained hidden for over 80 years and the royal biographer, Hugo Vickers, said that the film should not have appeared and that it was a stain on the Royal Family.

Follow the Rabbit-Proof Fence, by Australian Aborigine writer Doris Pilkington Garimara, was adapted for the big screen as "Rabbit-Proof Fence."[7] The drama depicts the Chief Protector of Aborigenes, Mr. Neville, implementing the Assimilationist policy to deal with the Aborigine issue and using the power conferred upon him to relocate half-caste children forcibly abducted from their mothers/families to educational centers. They were to be educated and trained as domestic servants and be given the culture of the white man in Jigalong Depot, Western Australia in 1931. Chapter 2 provides evidence of the secrecy pertaining to the "Stolen Generations."In 2010, Jim Loach, the son of British film-director Ken Loach, produced *Oranges and Sunshine*, a drama about the deportation from Britain of up to 150,000 children who had been shipped off to a "new life" in distant parts of the Empire, right up until 1970.[8]

American freelance journalist, Heather Brooke (2011, 16–33), charted systems implemented by the UK Government allegedly to protect children. There are over 11 million children under 18 in England (ONS 2014). Of these, over 390,000 children received support from children's services in

---

7 Philip Noyce, 2002. The French title is "Le Chemin de la liberté."

8 The film is based on Margaret Humphreys's book *Empty Cradles* [1994] which was reissued in 2011 as *Oranges and Sunshine*. Margaret Humphreys is the Director and founder of the Child Migrants Trust.

England last year, while over 49,000 children in England were identified as needing protection from abuse (DfE 2015). Although reports of sexual offences against children have increased sharply (NSPCC 2015), intrusive details about, for instance, children's obesity, behavior, and attendance records or assessment and profile—which seek to predict potential offenders—can be found in the databases. Information collected from behind closed doors stem from a report commissioned by the Joseph Rowntree Reform Trust Ltd (Anderson et al. 2009). In the wake of the loss of two discs by Her Majesty's Revenue and Customs that contained a copy of the entire child benefit database in 2007 and the subsequent front page headlines, experts convened to map the state of Britain's database, identifying the many public sector databases that collect personal information. Of the 46 databases assessed in the report, only 6 were found to have a proper legal basis for any privacy intrusions and are proportionate and necessary in a democratic society. Nearly twice as many are almost certainly illegal under Human Rights and Data Protection law and should be scrapped or substantially redesigned, while the remaining 29 databases have significant problems and should be subject to an independent review (Brooke 2011, 16–33). "Connexions," introduced by the Learning Skills Act 2000, to reduce the number of young people aged 16–18 who were not in education, employment, or training (Neets) was a controversed government pilot scheme providing education and work-related advice and guidance to support 13- to 19-year-old young people. Ultimately, it transpired that it recorded and shared teenagers' personal data with other agencies, which was forbidden under Section 537 of the Education Act 1996. Nowadays, The Common Assessment Framework (CAF) assesses and profiles young people in Britain with "no hidden agenda" (CAF 2014, 23).

Another sensitive and complex arena pervaded by secrecy is the use of animals in research. Activist groups and anti-vivisectionists have demanded an end to the secrecy surrounding animal testing. Former Huntingdon Life Sciences (HLS)—an unsuitable name as far as animals who live and die for medicine and commerce are concerned—has now been rebranded Envigo and is an organization based in the remote and secluded countryside of the Fens, in Occold near Eye, Suffolk, protected by security guards and barbed wires. Entry into the premises requires identity papers to be shown and checked. The organization, the largest contract research organization in the UK with nearly every major pharmaceutical firm in the world listed amongst its clients, has actually been using tens of thousands of animals in biomedical research annually. In mid-1997, when the Labour government first published proposals for freedom of information, the experimental laboratory of the organization was infiltrated and filmed undercover. It sparked huge controversy after the video footage was broadcast and revealed animal cruelty on top of the tests being administered. Some members of staff were prosecuted and dismissed, and a string of injunctions (e.g. not to approach the premises) were obtained.[9] The public then asked to have the right to know how and why animals were used in experiments in the name of scientific research. In 2000, Tony Blair's government passed The Freedom of Information Act, i.e. the right to have access to information held by public authorities. On May 1, 2014, the former coalition launched a 6-week public consultation into the repeal of the "secrecy clause" of the Animals (Scientific Procedures) Act 1986 (The Independent 2014)—the confidentiality clause of the UK law on animal experiments provides scientists who test on animals with a cloak of secrecy behind which to hide. The coalition was committed to reducing the use of animals in scientific research via the adoption of The 3Rs: (i) replacement of animals with non-animal methods as appropriate, (ii) reduction of the numbers of animals used, and (iii) refinement of procedures to minimize harm to animals involved were serving as a smoke screen to enable, for instance, dogs to be force-fed and other animals to suffer in tests and die. In the same year, an Ipsos MORI poll commissioned by the Department for Business, Innovation and Skills has shown that public opposition to the use of animals in medical testing has grown steadily over the past years. More than one in three people in the United Kingdom now identify themselves as "objectors" to the use of animals in medical research. An international campaign, Stop Huntingdon Animal Cruelty (SHAC), was launched with a view to closing down the Centre. Yet, they halted their 15-year-long animal rights campaigning in summer 2014. The last Labour Government made some positive progress for animals, including banning the use of animals in cosmetic products and tobacco tests, ending fur farming, and passing legislation to prohibit the use of hunting with dogs. There were also some measures in the Animal Welfare Act 2006 which were well-received.

But official secrecy continues despite the Government's publication of the Freedom of Information Act 2000 under Tony Blair, which amended the

---

9   First-hand information gathered by the author on two upsetting visits in Huntingdon Life Centre near Eye, to assess two biology-toxicology student work placements at the beginning of the 2000s, University of Nantes.

Data Protection Act 1998 and the Public Records Act 1958, with a view to implementing one of the Labour Party's manifesto promises to end a culture of secrecy in government. Many people have been left scarred for life following the abuse they were the victims of, and the "monstrous behaviour of the British Broadcasting Corporation (BBC), as 117 people thought and knew of rumors of sexual abuse and pedophilia being committed against both girls and boys by a presenter viewed as untouchable, Jimmy Savile,[10] now known to have been a predatory sex offender. Both Savile and the former broadcaster, Stuart Hall, used their fame to be friend and abuse the vulnerable and were thus able to go undetected for several decades, from 1959 to 2006. People were deluded by reputation and personalities, but the truth is now out and questions have been asked (Smith 2016). The BBC's alleged "culture of fear," which allowed abuse to go on for four decades, and enabled presenters to get away with those crimes for so long, could also be construed as a culture of secrecy. Mary Whitehouse, who started a moral crusade and campaigned against permissive society, founded The Clean Up Television campaign in 1964, which a year later became the National Viewers' and Listeners' Association. The BBC had always been her prime target.

This online publication has seven sections. The first chapter explores modern freemasonry, which emerged in Britain during the eighteenth century, combining earlier stonemason customs and methods of organization with the popular passion for clubs and societies. Although by no means unique in its ideology and constitution, freemasonry established itself after 1700 as a prominent fixture in both British communal and social life. Some mocked masonic lodges and their rituals, but they were an accepted feature on the social scene and, given that they avoided political and religious discussion and swore loyalty to the existing regime, their position was largely uncontroversial. The French Revolution, however, caused a severe backlash against the masons in Britain and Europe. During the 1790s, masonic lodges, which were once viewed simply as charitable and sociable organizations, were now seen as convenient vehicles for allowing radical groups to pursue covert revolutionary activities. As a result, legislation was passed which attempted to regulate these societies and eradicate any traces of secrecy. Despite its commitment to the establishment, freemasonry came under suspicion. The chapter examines the structure, nature, and characteristics of Scottish freemasonry in its wider British contexts between the years 1790 and 1799. In particular, it focuses on the Government's prejudicial

---

10 Sir James Wilson Vincent Savile (1926–2011).

and exploitative attempts to brand masonic lodges as hotbeds of secrecy within which attempts were made to subvert the constitution and foment rebellion. Masonic lodges and their members changed and adapted as these contexts evolved. Taking great pains to defend the fraternity against allegations of treason and sedition, reaffirm allegiance to the Government, and distance itself from the shroud of secrecy which had enveloped the society for centuries, the modern mason was forced to reconcile the desire to disabuse biased Government perceptions with the need to preserve the integrity of the association.

The second chapter addresses the question of the Stolen Generations in the Australian Northern Territory from the early 1900s to the late 1970s. The term "the Stolen Generations" was first coined in 1981 by Dr. Peter Read and is the phrase that the Aboriginal people have embraced for their collective tragedy —the separation of thousands of children of mixed descent from their mothers and communities throughout the country in the twentieth century. Despite having been lawful, these removals were conducted at random, based on race and most of the time under the veil of secrecy. The policemen or officers in charge of the removals took the children under duress, very often without any parental consent, or told them that they were taking their children for their own good to give them an education and a better start in life. The news quickly spread among the Aboriginal communities. Consequently, knowing that their children could be removed, the Aborigines decided to hide them or even sometimes put coal on their faces so that they were too dark to interest the policemen who were essentially looking for fair-skinned children who could be assimilated more easily into mainstream society. The members of the Stolen Generations were removed from their families, their tribal culture, and all other aspects that constituted their Aboriginality. They were forcibly made to adapt to, and embrace, a culture, whose codes were unknown to them and whose only aim was to cut them off from their native bonds and lie to them, brainwash them, punish them, or hide information and control every aspect of their private lives without any hesitation. Missionaries and superintendents who visited their homes did not hesitate to tell them that their parents were dead or even that they had been abandoned. Secrets, secrecy, and lies were part of the daily life of those children who were lost between two worlds and stuck in limbo. Once they were out of the camp, home, or institution, they had to face the truth, the harsh reality of their situation, and the consequences of the lies imposed upon them during all those years. They had to face the harshness of life in the "real world" without being armed for it so as to finally be able to go home.

The third chapter tackles the resignation of three Treasury Ministers in January 1958, which marked a break from Prime Minister Harold Macmillan's expansionist and Keynesian policies. The dispute over the 1% budget cut, amounting only to £100 million, undermined their credibility to control the money supply as a means to hold down inflation and preserve the position of sterling. Macmillan, who aimed to be seen as "Supermac"—nonchalantly able to guarantee prosperity, expansion, and materialism—dismissed the resignations as "little local difficulties." Since then, he had done his utmost to win the 1959 General Election through buying votes with promises of prosperity. He eventually did so with a landslide victory before being compelled to reappoint Enoch Powell in his government in 1960. The Treasury resignation has been much debated, but there have not yet been any studies to assess Powell's behind-the-scenes role and his motivations to resign. In addition, an analysis of the Powell papers at Churchill College, Cambridge, unveils a fresh narrative, which fills in some of the gaps in the historiography. As a matter of fact, Powell disclosed that he had secret reasons for resigning. As he was interested in pushing further his analysis on inflation, Powell engaged in a secret correspondence with an anti-Keynesian economist in Cambridge, Denis Robertson, to support the upsides of controlling the money supply —which would, to some extent, pave the way for Margaret Thatcher's monetarist policies of the 1980s. This chapter aims to unfold this new narrative by focusing on Powell's practice of secrecy, but also on his denunciation of it to avoid becoming a backbencher and to rejoin the government a couple of years later as a powerful senior figure in the Conservative Party. It will also provide a critical insight into Macmillan's "never-had-it-so-good" premiership in the late 1950s, as well as the myth of "Thatcherism *avant la lettre*."

Secrecy has characterized how Wales is governed ever since its sheer annexation by England in 1536. Any decision concerning the Welsh territory was made in London, in Westminster's or 10 Downing Street's dark corridors, and not openly in Cardiff, before being imposed on the local population. It was exactly in that way that at the end of 1955, the Welsh people were informed that Liverpool had secretly decided the building of a reservoir in Wales in order to provide its factories with water. The scheme implied to drown the Cwn Celyn Valley, near Tryweryn, and to move an important Welsh-speaking community. The local population was caught off guard by that totally unexpected decision. Wales thus suffered from a democratic deficit for many decades during which the Welsh people voted en masse for the Labour Party and yet had to be subjected to Margaret Thatcher's policy of market liberalization through the Secretaries of State for Wales who were both Conservative and very often English. This chapter aims to study how the British Government may have used secrecy in order to spare the Welsh periphery, to the detriment of democracy—a policy regularly denounced by the local press —and to consider the reasons why the Welsh government, which was committed to transparency, seems to have adopted the same practices.

In a democracy, the marriage of secrecy is defined as the ability and practice of keeping information hidden from the public or groups of people and only accessible to insiders, while politics is a term which describes the activities associated with the governance of a country. Such a combination is considered to be a bad match. Whether condemned as abuses of power or legitimized as measures of protection, political secrets have always been at the heart of the political process, even if calls for transparency, used in conjunction with claims for accountability, have been regularly issued, especially since the beginning of the twenty-first century. In the normal course of events, political secrets can only be assessed once they have been revealed, as they bring new and/or complementary pieces of information into the open, which allow for a better explanation and understanding of events and actions.

In British party politics, secrets and revelations are all the more significant when they are related to a third party, whose double aims are to put an end to the existing dual confrontation between the Labour and the Conservative Parties and to prove that they can be an efficient party of government. This chapter analyses how the Liberal Democrats in the United Kingdom have dealt with the intentional and unintentional disclosures of secret information about themselves and their rivals, concerning either the public or the private spheres. It evaluates the impact of such events on the party itself, its image, and its popularity.

A significant number of public scandals have recently confirmed the long-standing suspicions that a "culture of secrecy" pervades English police services. Inquiries into the deaths of 96 football supporters at the Hillsborough Football Stadium, and the police killings of Blair Peach, Jean Charles

De Menezes, and Ian Tomlinson, not to mention investigations into the numerous deaths of citizens detained in police custody, have revealed that the police consistently seek to manipulate the truth. They do so not simply to protect individual officers from prosecution, but also to promote a particular political agenda which entails the enforcement of state control over certain populations to the exclusion of others, highlighting the criminal behavior of the powerless while diverting public attention from the extensive harm perpetrated by the powerful. Indeed, as Reiner (2010) argues, policing must be understood as an inherently political form of action. The police help to construct a public narrative according to which the state and its institutions are justified in resorting to authoritarian methods in order to provide physical security for the public at large. Such a narrative deliberately conceals the state's own responsibility in creating the social and economic insecurity that has been exacerbated by over three decades of neoliberal capitalist policies. Current attempts on the part of the British state to "police the crisis" (Hall et al. 1978) of neoliberal capitalism represent a desperate attempt to stem the tide of unrest and seek legitimacy by scapegoating the most marginalized individuals for contemporary problems. This strategy risks being entirely counterproductive, as the institutionalized corruption within British policing is revealed to the public, undermining trust and confidence and calling into question the extent to which the police are capable of shoring up the power of the neoliberal state.

The final chapter presents the paradoxical co-existence of secrecy and transparency in the English justice system through the analysis of the concept of legal professional privilege (LPP). It starts by examining a definition of LPP as a protection from disclosure attached to the communications that took place between an individual and a legally consulted lawyer. It subsequently focuses on the two forms of LPP—legal advice privilege (LAP) and litigation privilege (LP)—two legal situations which, though not the same, grant immunity from compulsory disclosure to all privileged (i.e. confidential) communications. Finally, it concentrates on the legal requirements to acknowledge LAP, namely the fact that communications or other documents have to be made for the purposes of legal advice, and that advice has to be related to the rights, liabilities, obligations, or remedies of the client.

This chapter seeks to define the notion of legal professional privilege as it is asserted in England and Wales. There are, in fact, two forms of legal professional privilege: legal advice privilege protecting confidential communications between lawyers and their clients made for the purpose of giving or obtaining legal advice; the litigation principle securing the secrecy of communications between lawyers, clients, and their parties made for the purposes of actual or contemplated litigation.

CITED WORKS

Primary sources

Department for Education. 2015. Main tables B3 and C1 in Characteristics of Children in Need in England, 2014–15; Main table D4 in *Characteristics of children in need in England, 2014–15*.

Home Office. "Consultation of the Review of Section 24 of the Animals (Scientific Procedures) Act 1986." https://www.gov.uk/government/uploads/system/uploads/attachment_data/file/313410/Consultation_on_the_review_of_Section_24_of_ASPA.pdf (accessed February 13, 2015).

House of Commons. "Hansard Debates." *Animal Experiment*, March 19, 2003: Column 241WH-262 WH. http://www.publications.parliament.uk/pa/cm200203/cmhansrd/vo030319/halltext/30319h01.htm

ONS. 2014. Table MYE2 in *Population estimates for UK, England and Wales, Scotland and Northern Ireland, mid-2014*.

The National Archives. "Education Act 1996." http://www.legislation.gov.uk/ukpga/1996/56/section/537A

The National Archives. "Freedom of Information Act 2000." http://www.legislation.gov.uk/ukpga/2000/36/contents

Secondary sources

Aldrich, Richard. 2005. "The Secret State." In *The Companion to Contemporary Britain, 1939–2000*, eds. Paul Addison and Harriet Jones. Oxford: Blackwell Publishing.

Anderson, Ross, Ian Brown, Terri Dowty, Philip Inglesant, William Heath, and Angela Sasse. 2009. *Database State*. York: Joseph Rowntree Reform Trust Ltd. http://www.jrrt.org.uk/sites/jrrt.org.uk/files/documents/database-state.pdf

BBC. 2001. "A Controversial Laboratory."January 18. http://news.bbc. co.uk/2/hi/uk_news/1123837.stm

Bradford, Sarah. 2002. *Elizabeth: A Biography of Her Majesty the Queen*. London: Penguin Books.

Brooke, Heather. 2011. *The Silent State, Secrets, Surveillance and the Myth of Democracy*. London: Windmill Books.

Castell, Sarah, Anne Charlton, Michael Clemence, Nick Pettigrew, Sarah Pope, Anna

Quigley, Jayesh Navin Shah, and Tim Silman. Ipsos MORI, *Public attitudes to Science 2014*. March 2014. https://www.ipsos-mori.com/Assets/ Docs/Polls/pas-2014-main-report.pdf

Channel Four Television. 1997. "It's a Dog's Life. *Countryside Undercover*.

Cowden, Mhairi. 2012. "No Harm, No Foul': A Child's Right to Know Their Genetic Parents." *International Journal of Law, Policy and the Family* 26 (1): 102–126.

Eekelaar, John. 2006. *Family Law and Personal Life*. Oxford: Oxford University Press.

Foucault, Michel. 1994. *Histoire de la sexualité: Tome 1 La Volonté de savoir*. Paris Gallimard.

Humphreys, Margaret. 2011. *Oranges and Sunshine*. London: Corgi Book.

Jütte, Sonja, Holly Bentley, Dan Tallis, Julia Mayes, Natasha Jetha, Orla O'Hagen, Helen Brookes, and Nicola McConnell. 2015. "How Safe are Our Children?" National Society for the Prevention of Cruelty to Children. https://www.nspcc.org.uk/globalassets/documents/ research-reports/how-safe-children-2015-report.pdf

Loach, Jim. 2010. *Oranges and Sunshine*

Morgan, Tom & Reilly, Jonathan. 2015. "Their Royal Heilnesses". *The Sun*. 15 July.

Morris, Nigel. 2015. "Secrecy Over Animal Testing to be Ended." *The Independent*, February 16. http://www.independent.co.uk/news/uk/

politics/exclusive-secrecy-over-animal-testing-ended-with-public-right-to-know-9307954.html (accessed March 20, 2015).

Noyce, Phillip. 2002. "Le Chemin de la liberté."

Poliakoff, Stephen. 2003. "The Lost Prince." *BBC Video.*

Smart, Carol. 2009. "Family Secrets: Law and Understandings of Openness in Everyday Relationships." *Journal of Social Policy* 38 (4): 551–567.

Smart, Carol. 2010. "Law and the Regulation of Family Secrets." *International Journal of Law, Policy and the Family* 24 (3): 397–413.

Smith, Janet (Dame). 2016. "The Jimmy Savile Investigation Report."February 25. www.bbc.co.uk/bbctrust/dame_janet_smith

SOCIETY NOW. Autumn 2014, 3.

The Children Workforce Development Council. 2009. "Early Indentification, Assessment of Needs and Intervention. The Common Assessment Framework for Children and Young People: A Guide for Practitioners." Leeds. http://www.plymouth.gov.uk/caf_for_practitioners_national_guidance.pdf

CHAPTER 1

SCOTTISH FREEMASONS AND THE STRUGGLE FOR IDENTITY: RADICAL SCAPEGOATS OR REVOLUTIONARY EXTREMISTS?

Dr. Mark C. Wallace
Lyon College, Arkansas

During the first half of the eighteenth century, freemasonry was already an old-established part of Scottish and British culture. Although its secrecy sometimes evoked skeptical feelings, freemasonry did not normally provoke the extreme antimasonic attitudes prevalent in Europe. Its organization and development were such that it had always precluded any serious accusations of treason or sedition from the public and the government. As the second half of the eighteenth century progressed, however, and the French Revolution exercised a significant influence over political thought, British freemasonry was targeted by a suspicious government intent on monitoring the activities of secret societies. As such, heavy-handed legislation passed in the 1790s to stamp out radical groups transformed Scottish freemasonry from a convivial, charitable association into an organization characterized by intense political rivalries and power struggles.

The motivations behind the formation of popular societies were much more than just the opportunity to debate issues, discuss topics of interests, or engage in convivial celebrations. The unstated purpose of most eighteenth-century Scottish clubs was the verbalization of a Scottish viewpoint and the improvement of Scottish society (Emerson 1973, 121). Roger Emerson has suggested that during the early eighteenth century—amidst the growing realization of the need for professional education—the new population of the learned and educated "became numerous enough to change the institutional mix in the country" (Emerson 2003, 19). Although intellectual clubs had existed since the 1680s, a new emphasis was placed upon the structure and objectives of such societies.

Central to any analysis of freemasonry is its relation to other groups. Radical organizations, however, discussed a different range of topics, as these associations were often politically or religiously motivated. While clubs and societies appeared and thrived in Scotland during the 1700s, other nations boasted their own array of clubs and societies. After 1789, however, certain groups—for example, the United Scotsmen, United Irishmen, and London Corresponding Society (LCS)—assumed the mantle of political radicalism. Very little is known about the relationship between freemasonry and the British government during the late-eighteenth and early-nineteenth centuries. In exploring the ways in which freemasons reacted to the political stresses brought about by the onset of the French Revolution and the enactment of parliamentary legislation aimed at regulating secret societies, this article addresses an important yet largely unknown aspect of eighteenth-century freemasonry. This article will further outline the climate of growing hostility toward British and European freemasonry in the years leading up to and following the outbreak of the French Revolution, the alleged and actual links between radical organizations and the freemasons, and the impact of governmental legislation aimed at eradicating the perceived threats of secret and seditious societies on British freemasonry.

THE CHANGING NATURE OF FREEMASONRY

According to masonic historian F.R. Worts, British freemasonry during the years 1717–1780 has long been regarded as structurally weak and morally deficient (Worts 1965, 1). Scottish lodges, however, established and enforced rules and regulations to ensure proper organization. Worts's generalized discussion also neglects three very distinct and divergent periods in the history of Scottish freemasonry: 1700–1735, the pre-Grand Lodge era; 1736–1789, the formal establishment of the Grand Lodge, the emergence of freemasonry as a popular Enlightenment society, and the consolidation of Grand Lodge power; and 1790–1808, an era defined by the national impact of the French Revolution and the increased presence of a central governing masonic institution. Similar to John Money's classification of English freemasonry, this final period was characterized by a "complex balance between ultimately conflicting tendencies which temporarily coincided" (Money 1990, 255–256).[1] Freemasonry was forced—

---

1 John Money separates eighteenth-century English freemasonry into three main periods: 1717–1750, marked by the formation of a Grand Lodge and the establishment of London as the centre of masonic activity; 1751–1775, characterized by development and growth of freemasonry outside of London; and 1776–1800, distinguished by the suspicion surrounding clubs and societies.

as a result of the French Revolution—to reconcile the secrecy and mystery surrounding the society with an urgent need to appear open and loyal to the government.

During this final and significant phase, the entire nature of freemasonry changed. Although masons largely avoided political and religious discussions, the intense revolutionary struggles of the late-eighteenth and early-nineteenth centuries did stimulate several political conflicts. Other Scottish clubs and societies—such as the Fair and Intellectual Society—banned political discussions, especially during the turbulent years of the late-eighteenth century. And The Easy Club—apparently unnerved by affairs of state and endeavoring to ban their discussion at meetings—explicitly asserted that "the Club shall never be acters or intermedlers in politicks as a Society" (McElroy 1969, 17–18). In several instances, these fears manifested the vulnerability of associations to undesirable divisions created along political and party lines. Discussing the Select Society, Davis McElroy writes that at a time when "revolutionary ... feeling ran high and the fear of an explosion which would wreck the society was well founded as ensuing events proved," the majority of the members [of the Speculative Society] decided that it "should be cautious in admitting as subjects of discussion or debate, the political topics of the day" (18).

Contrary to the political skepticism of some organizations, others—for example the Scottish Dialectic and Logical Societies—permitted such discussions. At a meeting on December 10, 1791, the society debated the following question: "Will the Revolution of France be of more Advantage than disadvantage to Europe"? Ultimately, the members "decided unanimously in the affirmative" (114). When the Logical Society and the Juridical Society merged in 1797, the Logical Society flourished while the Juridical Society languished for one reason: the Logical Society permitted politically tinged discussions and the Juridical Society did not (130). Indeed, any society which discouraged such considerations would be unattractive to those potential members who wished to engage in political discussions. McElroy, however, notes that the "French Revolution and its consequences brought all political discussion among the young men in these debating societies under suspicion" (130).

Unfortunately for Scotland, the French Revolution was a watershed event in terms of the nature of Enlightenment sociability, and Michael Lynch astutely observes that the appearance of radical associations inspired by the

French Revolution ultimately threatened to expose the secrecy and rituals carefully crafted by clubs and societies. He further notes that

> The Select Society had faded in popularity at the seeming height of its influence, in the early 1760s. A generation later, the Speculative Society, home of most of the later literati, saw attendance at its meetings decline after 1789; the proposal in 1794, supported by Walter Scott and Francis Jeffrey, that the Society be allowed to discuss 'the political topics of the day', split it asunder. Politics had infiltrated the world of the clubs ... The unique atmosphere which for almost a century had stimulated and cosseted the brilliant world of the literati dissolved. (Lynch 2000, 350)

It was this infiltration that was responsible, as Lynch asserts, for the demise of various associations; it was also this intrusion that was to blame for the near-collapse of Scottish freemasonry. Although masons rejected political and religious discussions, politics soon became an integral part of the society. Pressured by a government intent on eradicating any traces of treason among clubs and societies in Britain, freemasons were forced to make politics a central issue.

CONSTITUTIONALISM, LOYALISM, AND POLITICS

The rise of politics coincided with an increase of loyalism as an expression of opposition to reformist organizations and, especially in the 1790s, "its more aggressive manifestations united around the war-cry 'Church and King!'" (Emsley 2000, 40). British freemasons were part of this loyalist upsurge and intensely emphasized their extreme patriotism and reverence for the "craft's sense of its own past, real and invented," and the "king as its symbol, head, and chief protector" (Melton 2001, 265–266).

This ideological support and trust in both the king and constitution played a vital role in establishing a political basis for lodges and contributed to a general standardization of laws and regulations. Lodge constitutions, texts, and rituals were all heavily influenced by proto-parliamentary themes such as electing officers by vote, discussing lodge business and issues in debates, imposing fines and penalties on members who violated rules, and keeping detailed minutes of all lodge transactions (258). James Van Horn Melton, assessing the political and ideological shift in British freemasonry, writes that

> By the 1790s ... freemasonry had become thoroughly domesti-
> cated. The rhetoric of liberty and brotherhood that had hitherto
> dominated the language of the movement gave way to a con-
> spicuously patriotic discourse, one that stressed respect for na-
> tional tradition and loyalty to church and king. Here the loyalist
> tone of British freemasonry mirrored more broadly the patriotic
> mood that pervaded British political culture at the end of the
> eighteenth century. (267)

This growth of loyalism was also apparent in Scotland. Speeches, prayers, and toasts that paid homage to the government and its leadership were of-ten extensively recorded in lodge minutes. For example, during a dedica-tion ceremony for the Barracks in Aberdeen in 1794, the Grand Chaplain of Scotland prayed that the building might "be so happily finished, as to become a commodious edifice for the temporary residence of British Sol-diers, the brave defenders of our King, our Constitution, our Religion, our liberties and our Laws" (Aberdeen Masonic Lodge No. 1(3) 1725–1810, June 24, 1794). Aberdeen Lodge No. 1(3) also equated freedom with the establishment. In a prayer given on July 7, 1801, at the laying of the founda-tion stone for the bridge over the Denburn River, the chaplain of the lodge prayed that the people might maintain their "Liberty, the happy order and good Government which we enjoy under our gracious King, our excellent Constitution and our equal laws" (June 24, 1794).

Masonic loyalism was also conveyed through letter writing. In correspon-dence, especially to the government and the king, freemasons expressed their sentiments about a variety of public issues and continually declared their intense support for the crown. A fine example is a letter of 1800 from the Grand Lodge of Scotland to George III after an attack had been made upon the king. Characterized by overzealous flattery and ornate language, the freemasons asserted their steadfast allegiance:

> We your Majesties most dutiful and Loyal Subjects The Grand
> Master and other officers of the Grand Lodge of Scotland with
> the Masters and Proxies of Lodge and their Wardens in Grand
> Lodge Assembled, approach your Majestys Throne with reflec-
> tion of Horror in common with all your other affectionate Sub-
> jects on the possible event of a recent attempt upon the Sacred
> person of your Majesty which but for the proof of that atrocity
> we should for the honour of humanity have doubted the reality.

The miserable person who made this wicked attack on a life so justly precious to the whole community must according to our feelings have either been vested by the Supreme Being with the greatest affliction to which our Nature is liable or be of a description of men (if such are entitled to the appellation) of which we are fully convinced there exists not another solitary Individual throughout the Extended Dominions of your Majesty.

The Magnanimity displayed by your Majesty on so trying an occasion will ever in recollection fill the eyes of your faithful Subjects with tears of gratitude as establishing your entire confidence on your affectionate People as having an effect pleasing. We are well aware to your Majesty of preventing many and serious mischiefs among the great concourse of your Subjects then assembled whose fears were alive for the safety of their beloved Sovereign. We take this opportunity of assuring your Majesty of the purity and simplicity of our Ancient order and of our sincere attachment to the Glorious Constitution of our Country founded on a basis which from its stability cannot be shaken by Foes foreign or Domestic, and conclude with our most anxious wishes for the long continuance and prosperity of your Majestys Reign, and for the permanent unimpaired and undisturbed felicity of your Majesty—and of every branch of your illustrious House. (Grand Lodge of Scotland 1795–1810, June 9, 1800)

Style and tone were carefully chosen and crafted in such a way as to portray freemasons as the most reliable supporters of church and state. Letters were even sent to the king congratulating him on the marriage of family members and on anniversaries of his accession. Such letters, however, were not exclusive to freemasons. Many organizations and public societies were "urged to send in loyal addresses to George III. More than 400 immediately did so, and many continued to at every excuse: by 1796 the King was sick of the sight of them, and ordered that they should be sent straight to [Henry] Dundas without bothering him" (Fry 1992, 168).

This outpouring of respect, however, was a new departure in the period after 1789. After all, Anderson's masonic *Constitutions* of 1723 stated that freemasons should be "resolv'd against all Politicks, as what never yet conduc'd to the Welfare of the *Lodge*, nor ever will" (Anderson 1976, 54). The Grand Lodge of Scotland recognized that "it was at all times unbecoming of them as a Body to interfere with Politics," but at the same it considered "Loyalty to the King and Submissions to the Laws to be duties incumbent On all" (Grand Lodge of Scotland, *Minutes*: November 30, 1795). Though such expressions of devotion strengthened public perceptions of the fraternity, the timing of their appearance suggests that the masons were attempting to bolster their image while simultaneously safeguarding themselves against government suspicion of them as members of secret societies.

REVOLUTIONARY ATTITUDES AND SUSPICION

Notwithstanding repeated affirmations of loyalty to the crown and the attempts of masons to proscribe political discussions, it is clear that some Scottish lodges were associated with radical and seditious societies. Freemasons in the United Kingdom espoused many divergent opinions and sentiments, and thus, it was quite possible that some supported political reform. Moreover, the fact that masons "met behind closed and guarded doors and deliberated in secret" linked them in some eyes with revolutionary societies in Britain and Europe (St Mungo's Lodge 1767–1810, November 4, 1788).

No. 8 Journeymen Operative Lodge in Edinburgh, for example, was involved in an incident which exemplified this gradual opening-up to political questions. On November 22, 1793, the lodge agreed to rent its premises for unspecified reasons to the radical organization the Society the Friends of the People. Led by their lionized and demonized vice president, Thomas Muir, and relying on Thomas Paine's *Rights of Man* (1791–1792) to express their beliefs in universal suffrage and annual parliaments, the Friends actively communicated with the LCS. The objectives of this radical body were to communicate with similar societies, promote its ideals, and—in extreme cases—foment rebellion. While it is not apparent that Muir was a freemason, he did correspond with Hamilton Rowan, who was a member of the First Volunteer Lodge of Ireland and Secretary of the Dublin Society of United Irishmen. E.W. McFarland suggests that one cannot rule out freemasonry "as an additional contact medium at this stage, given its role among other Enlightenment influences on radicalism" (McFarland 1994, 75).

In 1792, the Friends held their first Convention in Edinburgh. Shortly thereafter, during the King's Birthday Riots, effigies of Henry Dundas were burned and the Lord Provost's house was attacked by anti-government demonstrators (Stevenson 1989, 69). McFarland notes that although Scotland was pacific during the 1780s, the rising tide of revolutionary and reform societies in England swept northwards after 1789 causing numerous disturbances, leading Dundas to assert that the Friends were to blame for much of the unrest (McFarland 1994, 81–82). Dundas was so concerned about the action of the Friends, in fact, that he lamented the inefficacy of parliament in checking the "indiscriminate process of the association," and asserted it would ultimately "spread the fermentation of the Country to such a height, that it will be impossible to restrain the effects of them. They stop at nothing, it would appear they intend to either murder myself or burn my house" (81–82). Indeed, following the formation of The Friends of the People in July 1792, numerous societies began to appear in September 1792, such as the Dundee Friends of the Constitution and the Glasgow Associated Friends of the Constitution.

Propagating reformist ideas in imitation of the French, the radicalism of the Friends caused much alarm not only within the British government, but among masonic lodges as well. On November 4, 1793, the Grand Lodge of Scotland met to discuss the actions of Journeymen Operative Lodge No. 8. Thomas Hay, the Substitute Grand Master of Scotland, intimated that

> He understood some of the Lodges in and about this City had been in the practice of allowing certain persons styling themselves 'The Friends of the People' to assemble in their Lodges, whose deliberations it was said were of a turbulent and Seditious tendency, and from the station in life of the greatest part of the people composing these Meetings, these Lodges could reap but very little pecuniary aid towards their funds. Therefore he moved, that these Lodges be in future prohibited from allowing any such meetings to be held in their said Lodges of the delegation before Mentioned. (Grand Lodge of Scotland, *Minutes*, November 4, 1793)

After the Grand Lodge communication of November 4 was issued, the Journeymen met on November 22, 1793 "for the purpose of Considering A Minute of the Grand Lodge about letting the Lodge room to the Society of the Friends of the People" (Journeymen Masonic Lodge No. 8 1707–1810, November 22, 1793). After deliberating upon the Grand Lodge's decision, the members ultimately resolved, "That the Lodge room should be Let to the highest bidder and for that purpose to advertise it in the Edinburgh

News papers" (November 22, 1793). Notwithstanding the Grand Lodge's resolution, No. 8 Journeymen Operative Lodge allowed a meeting of the Friends to take place on December 5, 1793. Lord Provost Thomas Elder, accompanied by several constables, forcibly disbanded the meeting; shortly thereafter, numerous members of the Friends were arrested and charged with sedition (Seggie 1930, 83–87). On December 7, 1793, the Grand Lodge of Scotland held a meeting to discuss the conduct of Lodge No. 8. During the meeting,

> it was Represented by the Substitute Grand Master that the Journeymen Mason Lodge of Edinburgh ... had subjected their Lodge to persons calling themselves the 'Friends of the People', and wished to know how the Grand Lodge would dispose of the matter. Whereupon it was Resolved to call by public advertisement in the newspapers, a General Meeting of the Grand Lodge to Consider the Matter, and ordered Circular Letters should be sent to the whole members or Committee of the Journeymen Mason Lodge requesting their attendance upon Thursday next at seven o'clock in the Evening, which was accordingly done, and cards sent to that effect. (Grand Lodge of Scotland, *Minutes*, December 7, 1793)

Subsequently, the Grand Lodge suspended five members of Lodge No. 8 for permitting the Friends to meet on their premises. In an overtly magnanimous gesture, the Grand Lodge acknowledged that it would "repone the whole members, and admit them to their free stations in the Lodge, they always behaving properly in time coming agreeable to the rules of the Craft" (December 7, 1793).

The overall links between freemasonry and radicals are tenuous at best. No comprehensive membership rolls for the Friends of the People exist; thus, it is highly problematic to claim that freemasons were actively involved with the radical association. There is evidence, however, which suggests that at least *some* members of masonic lodges were affiliated with other radical groups. In Dundee, three members of St David's Lodge were involved with the Dundee Friends of Liberty and the Perth and Dundee Radical Society. Among the most famous members of the Friends of Liberty was George Mealmaker, who also was a leader of the United Scotsmen; Mealmaker was arrested in 1797 and tried for sedition (Ferguson 1965, 261). Among Mealmaker's colleagues in the Friends of Liberty were James Yeoman, baker, and a member of St David's Lodge (Gallin 1979, 249). Members of both the Perth and Dundee Radical Club and St David's masonic lodge include William Bisset, a "rich" founder, and one Mr. Crichton, who is listed in the *Chartulary and List of Lodges and Members: 1736–1799* as Patrick Crichton (Gallin 1979, 249; Grand Lodge of Scotland 1736–1799, 1736).[2] And in Edinburgh, James Thomason Callender—member of the Canongate and Leith, Leith and Canongate Lodge—is listed as a member of the radical Canongate No. 1 Society of the Friends of the People (Gallin 1979, 248). An outspoken critic of what he perceived as Britain's "imperialist foreign policy," (Brims 1993, 152), Callender published several pamphlets agitating for parliamentary reform and a return of the British constitution to "its original purity" (152).

Robert Burns, freemason and member of St David's Tarbolton and Canongate Kilwinning Lodges, suffered from what McElroy calls "revolutionary fever" (McElroy 1969, 100–101). During the 1790s, appetites increased among young Scottish men for revolutionary literature and often such curiosity placed them "in social and political hot water" (100–101). Burns admired Tom Paine, and briefly entertained the idea of joining the Friends of the People although there is no clear evidence linking him with the radical group. It seems as if the revolutionary fervor aroused the political sentiments of Burns, not the masonic lodges of which he was a member.

As we have seen, those few masons who were sympathizers with reformers or known radicals, and the incident involving No. 8 Journeymen Lodge and the Friends of the People do not, of course, definitively link Scottish freemasons with radical and subversive societies. It does, however, suggest that the members of St David's Lodge, Canongate and Leith, Leith and Canongate Lodge, St David's Tarbolton Lodge, and Canongate Kilwinning Lodge were susceptible to the ideas of reformist groups. And certainly, the members of the Journeymen Lodge No. 8 were familiar with the Friends, as that society had held conventions in Edinburgh and the arrest and trial of Thomas Muir was a much-publicized event in the city.

The altercation between No. 8 Lodge and the Grand Lodge of Scotland typifies the tensions present between the Grand Lodge, its lodges, and the government during the final years of the eighteenth century. In the politi-

2 See also Corey Andrew Edwards, "Paradox and Improvement: Literary Nationalism and Eighteenth Century Scotland Club Poetry," unpublished Ph.D. thesis (Ohio: 2000), 97.

cally volatile climate of the 1790s, it was imperative that the Grand Lodge demonstrates its intolerance of insubordination and reaffirms the loyalty of freemasons to church and state. As the concerted effort to stamp out revolutionary threats and treasonable societies increased, however, the Grand Lodge's ability to settle these disputes was impaired by a conflict of interests: wanting to appear strong in the face of discord, yet at the same time not wanting to alienate constituent lodges and bring about further controversy. The decision by No. 8 Journeymen Lodge to allow the Friends to meet on their premises also manifests two further trends: the inability of the Grand Lodge to enforce its decisions and the propensity of lodges to act on their own accord. Indeed, these two patterns greatly reinforced the role of the Grand Lodge of Scotland as a figurehead of Scottish masonry, not a central ruling body. As such, it was ill prepared to defend freemasons in general against the swirl of revolutionary accusations that surfaced during the last years of the eighteenth century.

The debate over masonic sympathies with revolutionary sentiments and support for radical activities has been taken up by many historians. According to historian Margaret Jacob, Jacobite sympathies may have existed in some British lodges, although they were much more prominent in Continental lodges (Jacob 1991, 54). Michael Kennedy argues that there is no proof to substantiate the influence of French masonic lodges on the French Revolution; he does, however, concede that "one cannot deny that the clubs owed much to the lodges" in terms of the emulation of rituals and general organizational structure (Kennedy 1982, 5–8). Contrary to such views, Thomas Munck maintains that "although the Masons did promote international and cross-social contacts which were essentially non-religious and in agreement with enlightened values," they can hardly be described "as a major radical or reformist network in their own right" (Munck 2000, 70). Notwithstanding varying perceptions of freemasonry, it is clear that by the 1790s freemasonry's turbulent and increasingly controversial existence in Europe had undermined confidence that British freemasonry was neither a subversive nor revolutionary organization.

Such controversies also included questions over the political aims of the society and the extent to which its actions and deliberations might be influenced by seditious European organizations. Freemasonry, as it appeared in Europe, was "first articulated in postrevolutionary Britain" and the "form of the lodge became one of the many channels that transmitted a new political culture, based upon constitutionalism, which gradually turned against traditional privileges and established, hierarchical authority" (Jacob 1991, 51). In Europe, Jacob argues, freemasonry did play a major role in nurturing and promoting revolutionary ideas. Although built upon the British model, Continental freemasonry had become politically and socially subversive and posed a clear threat to all forms of organized religion:

> Whether we are examining the literature of British Freemasonry ... or entering individual lodges on the Continent ... one major point needs to be stressed: these were political societies, not in a party or faction sense of the term but in a larger connotation. Within the framework of civility and in the service of an imagined social cohesion, the lodges practiced a civil administration, derived from British political practice and tradition. Predictably in a British context lodges were, on the whole, remarkably supportive of established institutions, of church and state. Yet they could also house divisive, or oppositional political practices. They could be loyalist to the Hanoverian and Whig order, yet they could also at moments show affiliation with radical interests, whether republican or Jacobite, and, possibly by the end of the century, Jacobin. Whatever the political affiliations of their members, the eighteenth-century masonic lodges were at the heart of a new secular culture, created in the century and fashioned to operate within the confines of its social ranks, privileges, and degrees. (50–51)[3]

Despite Jacob's assertions, Jeremy Black maintains that although some cynics perceived freemasonry to be a dissident faction intent on fomenting radical activities and, occasionally, blamed the society for the French Revolution, most lodges existed purely for sociable reasons. The lodges were, to be sure, "no more radical in practice than several other aspects of European thought in this period" (Black 1999, 496–497).

Masonic historian David Stevenson correctly reasons that frequent misuse of the word "masonic" to describe "anything combining radical ideas and secrecy ... was illogical and confusing" (Stevenson 1988, 1–12). This confusion ultimately allowed critics of the masons to formulate conspiracy theories which asserted that "freemasonry was one of the great causes of the

---

3   See also Robert Clifford, *Application of Barruel's Memoirs of Jacobinism, to the Secret Societies of Ireland and Great Britain* (London: 1798), 1–50.

French Revolution" (Jacob 1991, 9–10). Although there was little tangible evidence to substantiate such allegations, British freemasonry became the object of much scrutiny and suspicion.

Several works published during the 1790s certainly contributed to the whole European paranoia pertaining to secret societies, more especially freemasons and the Illuminati. Among these publications was Abbe de Barruel's work titled *Memoires pour server a l'Historie de Jacobinisme*, or *Memoirs, Illustrating the History of Jacobinism* (1798). Although his book cast freemasons in unfavorable terms, Barruel did attempt to distinguish between British and French freemasonry, separating their goals, aims, and practices. In *Memoires*, Barruel notes that "England in particular is full of those upright men, who, excellent Citizens, and of all stations, are proud of being Masons, and who may be distinguished from the others" (Barruel 1798, 273). Barruel engages in a discursive and somewhat rambling exegesis of masonic orders, rites, and rituals, and concludes that the occult—or higher orders—of freemasonry teach those mysteries and principles "which operated the French Revolution" (398). Michael Kennedy dismisses Barruel's claims, stating that

> A tremendous amount of research has been done in recent years on freemasonry; and while, unfortunately, only a small proportion pertains directly to the clubs, it is now possible to discard a number of once-popular theories about their masonic origins. Today, only the most imaginative minds could describe the masons as conspirators who established the clubs as part of a grand design to subvert the Church and the Monarchy. (Kennedy 1982, 8)

Controversial as it might seem, Barruel's work candidly revealed the suspicion surrounding secret orders and societies. Although at times representing shadow as substance, it nevertheless provided a framework for those convinced that all of Britain stood on the brink of revolution based on the French model and that secret societies throughout Europe were conspiring to overturn governments and inspire social upheaval.

It was, perhaps, a work by an Edinburgh professor which had the most influence on the Scottish attitude to the masons in the later 1790s. In 1797, amid claims of Jacobin lodges in France and seditious and treasonable activities among German freemasons, John Robison—eminent mechanical philosopher and professor of natural philosophy at the University of Edinburgh—published *Proofs of a Conspiracy Against All the Religions and Governments of Europe, Carried on in the Secret Meetings of the Freemasons, Illuminati, and Reading Societies, Collected from Good Authorities* (Robison 1797). Despite Robison's titular assurances that the sources for his information were inherently trustworthy, W. K. Firminger argues that Robison was seized by a panic that "the whole system of society was in progress of demolition by the French Revolution," and thus he "strayed from more accordant subjects to look for the causes of all the confusion" (Firminger 1937, 31–69). Ultimately, he traced alleged conspiratorial crimes to the machinations of freemasons:

> Being at a friend's house in the country during some part of the summer 1795, I there saw a volume of a German periodical work, called *Religions Begebenheiten, i.e.* Religious Occurrences; in which there was an account of the various schisms in the Fraternity of Free Masons, with frequent allusions to the origin and history of that celebrated association. This account interested me a good deal, because, in my early life, I had taken some part in the occupations (shall I call them) of Free Masonry; and having chiefly frequented the Lodges on the Continent, I had learned many doctrines, and seen many ceremonials, which have no place in the simple system of Free Masonry which obtains in this country ... I had also remarked, that the whole was much more the object of reflection and thought than I could remember it to have been among my acquaintances at home. There, I had seen a Mason Lodge considered merely as a pretext for passing an hour or two in a sort of decent conviviality, not altogether void of some rational occupation. I had sometimes heard of differences of doctrines or of ceremonies, but in terms which marked them as mere frivolities. But, on the Continent, I found them matters of serious concern and debate ... But all the splendour and elegance that I saw could not conceal a frivolity in every part. It appeared a baseless fabric, and I could not think of engaging in an occupation which would consume much time, cost me a good deal of money, and might perhaps excite in me some of that fanaticism, or, at least, enthusiasm that I saw in others, and perceived to be void of any rational support. (Robison 1797, 1–3)

Robison himself had been initiated in Lodge La Parfaite Intelligence at Liège in March 1770. Despite his masonic affiliations, he believed that Continental freemasonry, as was particularly found in Germany and France, was potentially subversive. His doubts were first circulated in the *Anti-Jacobin Review*, a conservative and loyalist monthly journal to which he regularly contributed. Similar to the ideas espoused in *Proofs of a Conspiracy*, the *Anti-Jacobin* "set out to refute what it considered to be the dangerous doctrines of sedition being fervently circulated in the country" (Emsley 2000, 18).[4] Robison did not directly accuse British freemasons of being seditious, but he remarked that:

> The homely Free Masonry imported from England has been totally changed in every country of Europe, either by the imposing ascendancy of French brethren, who are to be found everywhere, ready to instruct the world; or by the importation of the doctrines, and ceremonies, and ornaments of the Parisian Lodges. Even England, the birth-place of Masonry, has experienced the French innovations; and all the repeated injunctions, admonitions, and reproofs of the old Lodges, cannot prevent those in different parts of the kingdom from admitting the French novelties, full of tinsel and glitter, and high-founding titles. (Robison 1797, 9)

Although he asserted that British masonic lodges were vehicles only for passing the time in merriment, Robison nevertheless retained some suspicions regarding their association with radical groups. He does note that no definitive link exists between European and British lodges, but Robison does not dismiss the possibility that Continental ideas of revolution did penetrate the British masonic models of constitutionalism and loyalism.

THE THREAT OF "ILLUMINISM"

A major cause of this change of opinion was the Order of Illuminati, founded by Adam Weishaupt in May 1776 in Bavaria. Weishaupt was a student at the University of Ingolstadt and by the age of 22, he was elected Professor of Canon Law of the same University, a position long held by Jesuits. It was

---

4   For an in-depth discussion of Jacobinism, see Augustin Cochin, "The Theory of Jacobinism," in *Interpreting the French Revolution*, ed. Francois Furet (Cambridge: 1981), 164–204.

his hatred of the Jesuits which ultimately formed the ideological foundation of the order he founded. Initially styled the Order of Perfectibilists and later changed to the Illuminati, the main goal of the society was to eradicate political and religious tyranny while simultaneously emphasizing morality and virtue (Black 1999, 399–400).[5] This program for restructuring society became known as Illuminism, which Weishaupt attempted to blend with freemasonry to ensure his Order's success. Ostensibly to dispel any doubts as to the aims of the Illuminati, he joined Lodge Theodore of Good Counsel in Munich in 1777. His radical political stance drew criticism, however, and the Order's association with freemasonry encouraged detractors' efforts to increasingly tarnish the reputation of the masons.

This was why The Order of the Illuminati was cited during the debate over the Secret Societies Act of 1799, which will be discussed in further detail. The suspicions the Illuminati provoked stemmed from their beliefs as well as their secrecy, and in an age "bred on notions of conspiracy, it is not surprising that Freemasonry and other movements aroused acute fears" (399–400). The Earl of Radnor expressed his skepticism about the activities of the freemasons, asserting that

> Their meetings were, in other countries at least, made subservient to the purposes of those Illuminati who had succeeded in the overthrow of one great government, and were labouring for the destruction of all others. This he conceived to have been proved in a work some time since published by a very learned Professor [Robison] and he was desirous to guard against any similar practices in this country. (Prescott 2000, 8)

Questioning the integrity of the society, Radnor further declared that "not being himself a mason, and having heard that they administered oaths of secrecy," he did not know "whether in times so critical as the present, it was wise to trust the freemasons any more than any other meetings" (8). Although the masons, as we have seen, professed their loyalty to the crown, some doubts still lingered in parliament about their reliability and allegiance.

---

5   Black writes that "in 1785 all secret societies, including the Freemasons and Illuminati, were banned by Karl Theodor of Bavaria and in 1787 evidence that purported to demonstrate a plot by the latter was published ... In an age bred on notions of conspiracy, it is not surprising that Freemasonry and other movements aroused acute fears ...," *Eighteenth-Century Europe*, 399–400.

It was this alleged connection between the Illuminati and freemasonry and the geographical reach of its influence which aroused the suspicions of Robison as well as James Robertson, a Benedictine monk in Galloway—so much so, in fact, that they each wrote to the Lord Advocate Robert Dundas. Robison warned Dundas of the potential subversive influence not only of the Illuminati, but European freemasons as well:

January 1798

My Lord

What I wished to inform your Lordship of is thus some time ago an invitation was given to the Fraternity of Free Masons in Scotland to hold a Correspondence with the Grand or Royal Lodge of Berlin. This was decorated with every Ornament and full of pompous titles, and conceived in terms of the highest import for Scotch Masonry. It was conceived as particularly addressed to the most advanced Order of Masonry (tho' I rather suppose it addressed to the National Lodge). This is supposed to be what they call the Royal Order of St. Andrews—professing what they call the Masonry of Rose Croix Tau the Letter, and thus it was from a Lodge professing the same Masonry. The simplicity of the fraternity in this Country has made us indifferent as to all the parties on the Continent, but of late we are also seized with the desire of innovation, and becoming fond of the high degrees of masonry. But we are quite ignorant of the life made of them abroad. I know that this System was continued by Swedes and the Duke of Sudermannia had a great hand in it. Under the most inoffensive exterior, I know that the cosmopolitical doctrines are most zealously taught, and that the whole of this Order is engaged in the Schisms of Illumatism. I firmly believe that this Invitation to a Correspondence is with a view to make proselytes. It were to be wished that it could be prevented. One way occurs to me, to publish the whole secrets of the Order, which are in my possession, but this is very disagreeable to me, because altho' I came under no obligation to consult them, the person who sent them to me, when he quitted Russia in haste, expected that they would be kept.

What makes me trouble your Lordship just now is the Letter which accompanies this. By it you will see that it is highly probably that a bad use is already made of Free Masonry in this Country. I remember hearing of the story of a detachment being spared by the French because they were Brethren but it was not supposed to be authentic by the foreign [illegible]. It would be of some use to inquire of our officers who were on the spot such as Major Tytler now at Stirling who was then an Aid de Camp, and must have known more than an ordinary battalion officer. If the Story could be proved to be false, it might put an End to the use made of it in Galloway and probably in other places.

I have sent your Lordship a pamphlet which I had a few weeks ago from Lord Auckland which confirms my Suspicions about the Swedish Masonry. I am respectfully

Your Lordships ms. Obedt. Servt.,
[Signed] John Robison[6]

Robertson's letter in January 1798 addresses issues similar to those raised by Robison. Robertson had attended seminary in Ratisbon, Germany, and after he was professed in 1778 he served on missions in Buchan, Edinburgh, and Galloway (Dilworth 1958, 191). Having briefly revisited Ratisbon in 1788, he returned to Scotland in 1789. By 1797, he was in Galloway when he composed the following letter to Dundas, which drew upon his recent and personal knowledge of Continental freemasonry:

My Lord,

Permit a Stranger to congratulate you & the world on your late performance. If anything can save us, it can only be men who have courage to unmask such horrors, at no small risk to their own lives. Providence I trust will work for the preservation of such useful Persons.

The writer of this happened to be at Ratisbon in the year 1788 when the discovery of illumination was quite fresh. I was told that one of those wretches had been struck dead with lightning

6   Letter from John Robison, (Laing MSS II 500), reprinted with the permission of the University of Edinburgh Library.

& that it was by papers found on him the discovery was made. They shew'd me the tree where he was thunderstruck. A Singular interposition of Providence, I pass'd afterwards by Munich where I was presented with the System & Correspondence published by the Elector's Authority: which I brought to Edinburgh where I think I lent it to Lord Elliock. But nobody there would believe it they treated it as a dream of the senseless Bavarians. I was laugh'd at in Munich, when I maintain'd that Scotch Masonry was not tinctured with Illumination. They assur'd me they had proof of a Correspondence with Scotland. In Galloway where I now live I can assure you Sir, that the Masons are uncommonly active in recruiting, having frequent & numerous meetings: they scruple at nobody however worthless which shews no good design. I believe the bulk of them is led by the nose but there is nothing good at bottom. I have this from very good Authority, that the Masons give out that when the Robespierrists had pass'd a decree to give no quarter to the English, a whole Regiment was saved by Masonry. I think it is said of the Inniskilling Dragoons, They were surrounded, as the story goes, by the French & were going to be cut to pieces, when the commanding officer stept forward & made some of the Mason's signs to the French, which their Commander observed & return'd: then the firing ceas'd & both parties retreated.

The circulation of this tale by the Masons to procure recruits has an obvious meaning, & therefore I presum'd it not unworthy [of] your notice. I think I had once the honor of being presented before your Couch, but you must have forgot that long ago ere now. May you arise from it more vigorous than ever & the health of your body equal the power of your mind.

I am with the most sincere Veneration

Sir Munches near   Your most obedt. Sert.
Dumfries 8 Jan.   [Signed] James Robertson <u>Priest</u>
1798[7]

---

7   Letter from James Robertson (Laing MSS II 1769–1770) reprinted with the permission of the University of Edinburgh Library.

Both Robison and Robertson clearly refer to the same military incident. Although they each were at pains to vindicate British freemasons, they do hint at the possibility of subversive activities on the West Coast of Scotland.

THE GOVERNMENT CRACKDOWN

Between the years 1792 and 1799, Parliament took the war against radicalism to a new level. Faced with perceived threats from subversive organizations and a dramatic increase of revolutionary sentiments in Britain, the government launched a campaign to eradicate all traces of sedition, treason, and sympathy for reformist societies. This assault—with both Prime Minister William Pitt and Henry Dundas at the vanguard—proved to be an intimidating political juggernaut.

Some historians, however, take a milder view of Pitt. Michael Duffy suggests that Pitt earnestly believed that any discontent would ultimately be thwarted by the reactionary and draconian measures taken by the government. Roger Wells dismisses the "blinkered approach" of those liberal historians who claim that no revolutionary threat existed or was, at best, marginal (Wells 1983, 45). Yet he also is skeptical of claims that Pitt's apparent paranoia was based on "fears of what might occur rather than what was actually happening" (45). Dogged by ethical quandaries and a reluctance to pursue any course of action that would infringe upon personal liberty and freedom, Pitt was acutely aware that any legislative measures had to be justified in terms of their necessity to preserving order and stability. According to Duffy, Pitt declared it his "mild and forgiving policy to separate the misguided from the criminal," (Duffy 2000, 150–152), a characterization which stands in marked contrast to comparisons of the Prime Minister to Robespierre.[8]

Pitt's first method of implementing this repressive policy was to "utilise existing disciplinary mechanisms as strongly as possible" (O'Gorman 1989, 30). This meant involving the magistrates and warning them in 1792 to monitor any seditious literature and to prevent—and if necessary, quell—any disturbances. Pitt also created a system of local informants and spies to monitor public mood and sentiments. The second method of policy enforcement was the exploitation of the legal system. Intent on setting an

---

8   See John Barrell, *Imagining The King's Death: Figurative Treason, Fantasies of Regicide 1793–1796* (Oxford: 2000), 18.

example through the harsh sentences imposed on prominent radical figures, Pitt was successful in intimidating and forcing into submission numerous seditious leaders. Through harassment, threats, and prosecutions,
Pitt's policy achieved its goal of stamping out popular dissent. The "*third
and complementary element in the government's repressive reaction to
domestic radical agitation: its use of Parliament and parliamentary enact-
ments*", however, had the most significant impact on radical societies and
the freemasons (32).

The first piece of legislation designed by the government for the purpose
of regulating clubs and societies was The Friendly Societies Act of 1793,
which allowed the government to monitor organizations in Britain. Under
the terms of the Act, clubs and societies had to be registered as benefit and
philanthropic associations. Ostensibly, the government justified the Act
as a means to create a list of friendly societies. In practice, however, the
Friendly Societies Act allowed the government to scrutinize the activities
of the associations. Membership lists that had to be submitted to the government provided personal information on each affiliate, thus giving officials a wealth of personal information as the Pitt administration waged its
war against seditious activities.

The Friendly Societies Act was discussed in Aberdeen Lodge No. 1(3). In
a minute dated 6 December 1793, the lodge recorded the following extract
which was also advertised in the *Aberdeen Journal*:

> The said day there was laid before the meeting by the Commit-
> tee Appointed by the Society for drawing up Rules and Regu-
> lations in terms of the late Act of Parliament for the relief and
> protection of Friendly Societies, a Report of said Committee
> with a copy of Rules, orders and Regulations to be observed in
> future by this said Society And which orders, Rules and regu-
> lations having been read over to the Meeting and deliberately
> considered, were by a very great Majority Approven of And the
> Lodge Did and do hereby make, ordain, and constitute the said
> Rules, which are hereby appointed to be engrossed in this Seder-
> int book as Constitutional and Fundamental Laws, Orders, and
> Regulations of this Society, to be observed in all time coming.
> Repealing hereby, and Rescinding all former Rules, Orders, and
> Regulations made and Established in this Society. (Aberdeen
> Masonic Lodge No. 1(3), December 6, 1793)

Although lodges such as No. 1(3) Aberdeen readily accepted the stipulations of the Act, its existence as a secret society made it and other lodges susceptible to any legislation aimed at preventing the meeting of any organizations with real or imagined treasonable or seditious purposes.

The one-two punch of Pitt and Dundas, combined with a formidable array of laws aimed at crushing radical sympathies and the pre-emptive strike at would-be agitators, proved to be intimidating, although the efficacy of such measures is questionable. Regardless, it has been argued that men such as Pitt and Dundas were "actuated almost entirely by interest and ambition" (Barrell 2000, 18 n.60). Similar to Pitt, Henry Dundas recognized the "evident signs ... of a very turbulent and pernicious spirit having pervaded numerous and various descriptions of persons" in Britain (Fry 1992, 159). He endorsed swift action against radical societies, suggesting that "whatever is to be done, ought to be done right" (159) and engaged in a "general witch-hunt against anyone tainted with dissent" (172). Although his campaign in England to suppress revolutionary societies is hardly remembered, in Scotland he is remembered as an "ogre of repression," (154) as Dundas strove to enforce the laws with stringent effect.

Ultimately, government initiatives and legislation such as the Friendly Societies Act paved the way for the most serious threats to freemasonry: the Unlawful Oaths and the Secret Societies Acts. Whether excessive or inspired by untenable threats, it is clear that more legislation in stricter and much harsher forms resulted from the inadequacy of earlier measures. The government passed the Unlawful Oaths (1797) and Secret Societies (1799) Acts, although the Secret Societies Act proved to be the more problematical of the two for freemasonry. The Unlawful Oaths Act, though, was significant, for the swearing of oaths was the basis by which the working class organized successfully and ensured both secrecy and solidarity. Fearing that such assemblies would incite revolutionary activities, the Unlawful Oaths Act stipulated that

> Any person is guilty of a felony and liable to heavy punishment who in any manner or form administers or causes to be administered, or aids or assists at, or is present and consents to the administering or taking of any oath or engagement purporting or intended to bind the person taking it to engage in any mutinous or seditious purpose, or to disturb the public peace, or to be of any society formed for such a purpose or to obey the orders of

any committee or body not lawfully constituted, or of any commander not having authority by law for that purpose, or not to
inform or give evidence against any associate or other person or
not to reveal any unlawful combination or any illegal act done
or to be done or any illegal oath or engagement or its import,
or who takes any such oath without being compelled to do so.
(Lambert 1975, 433–435)

While masonic initiations involved compulsory oaths and obligations, they
were not seditious or mutinous. Ultimately, the freemasons were not directly implicated under this Act. To allay suspicion, however, the Grand Lodge
of Scotland and the Ancient Grand Lodge of England resolved "To hold no
procession on St Andrews Day, and it was recommended to Brethren, who
might visit one another on the occasion, to pass as privately through the
streets as possible, so that there might be no cause given for raising a tumult
or noise in the street (Lindsay 1935, 246).

In addition to prohibiting all public masonic processions, the Ancient
Grand Lodge of England determined that

It be recommended to His Grace the Duke of Atholl Right Wor-
shipful Grand Master of Free Masons of England according to
the Old Constitutions to inhibit and totally prevent all public
Masonic Processions—and all private meetings of Masons of
Lodges of Emergency upon any pretence whatsoever and to
suppress and suspend all Masonic Meetings except the regular
stated Lodge Meetings and Royal Arch Chapter which shall
be held open to all Masons to visit duly qualified as such. That
when the usual Masonic Business be ended the Lodge shall then
disperse, the Tyler withdraw from the Door of the Lodge room
and formal restraint of Admission shall cease. The above Resolu-
tions being submitted to this Committee they were unanimously
approved of and confirmed. Ordered that the Grand Secretary
shall immediately give Notice to every Lodge under the Ancient
Constitution also to the Grand Lodges of Scotland and Ireland
... of these proceedings. (Ancient Grand Lodge of England
1786–1810, May 6, 1799)

The immediate effects of the legislation were minimal at best, only calling
into question the secrets contained within and the substance of masonic

oaths. It did not insinuate that freemasons shared the radical tendencies of such factions as the Friends of the People and the LCS. Two years later, however, freemasonry would be directly affected by the passage of the Secret Societies Act, the most "sweeping of the legislative measures introduced by Pitt's government to forestall the threat of a revolution" (Prescott 2000, 1). In a speech delivered to the House of Commons on April 19, 1799, Pitt listed the names of those radical associations that he believed posed the greatest risk to domestic stability, including clubs and societies such as the freemasons that were secretive by nature. By name, the government outlawed the LCS, the United Englishmen, United Scotsmen, United Irishmen, and the United Britons. Pitt justified the legislation by emphasizing the continual need to oppose seditious societies:

> We must proceed still farther, now that we are engaged in a most important struggle with the restless and fatal spirit of Jacobinism, assuming new shapes, and concealing its malignant and destructive designs under new forms and new practices. In order to oppose its effect, we must also from time to time adopt new modes, and assume new shapes ... These marks are wicked and illegal engagements of mutual fidelity and secrecy by which the members are bound; the secrecy of electing the members; the secret government and conduct of the affairs of the society; secret appointments unknown to the bulk of the members; presidents and committees, which, veiling themselves from the general mass and knowledge of the members, plot and conduct the treason—I propose that all societies which administer such oaths shall be declared unlawful confederacies. (3)

By July 1799, the government had passed the Secret Societies Act, or "An act for the more effectual suppression of societies established for seditious and treasonable purposes; and for the better preventing treasonable and seditious practices," which effectively regulated and policed freemasonry in Scotland. In no uncertain terms, the Act emphatically declared that

> A traitorous conspiracy had long been carried on with the persons from time to time exercising the power of government in France to overturn the laws, constitution and government and that in pursuance of such design, diverse societies had been instituted ... All and every of the said societies [that require] an

unlawful oath or engagement ... shall be deemed guilty of an unlawful combination and confederacy. (Lambert 1975, 365–384)

Although arguably masonic oaths were not seditious, stipulations set forth
by the Act demanded public initiations which would immediately result in
the forced exposure of masonic oaths, rites, and rituals.

By July 1799, freemasons in both England and Scotland were guaranteed
protection from the Secret Societies Act, as Prime Minister Pitt "expressed
his good opinion of the Society and said he was willing to recommend any
clause to prevent the new act from affecting the Society, provided that the
name of the society could be prevented from being made use of as a cover
by evilly disposed persons for seditious purposes."[9] And it is highly likely
that the aristocratic leadership of Lord Moira, the Duke of Atholl, and Sir
James Stirling helped the freemasons escape charges of sedition.[10]

Despite such a favorable outcome, continued masonic emphasis on charity
and self-improvement did little to bolster its image or position among the
upper-echelons of the government. Although it was eventually reclassified
as an organization unlikely to pose a threat to the stability of the country, it
suffered much at the hands of the legislation. Fewer lodges were chartered
throughout the 1790s, and accompanying the reduction in lodge numbers was a concomitant decrease in new members and overall decline in
charitable funds. Furthermore, masonic autonomy was compromised, as
it—more specifically the Grand Lodge of Scotland—now answered to the
national government.

CONCLUSION

Historians have questioned the strength of radicals in Scotland as well as
the legitimacy and the overall impact of the repressive legislation. Fry comments that

> Scotland's history contained little preparation for a secular radical-
> ism. Previous accounts, seeking its roots, have too glibly lumped

---

9   Cited in Prescott, "Unlawful," taken from Library and Museum of Freemasonry, Minutes of the Hall Committee Minute Book No. 4, July 23, 1799.

10 Lord Moira was the Acting Grand Master of the Grand Lodge of England, Atholl the
Grand Master of the Ancient Grand Lodge of England,, and Stirling the Grand Master
of Scotland.

it together with the reforming movements in counties and burghs, as part of a universal democratic awakening ... Reformers, in contradistinction to radicals, owed nothing to foreign revolutionary inspiration ... The radicals were unsuccessful in rousing the masses with them. (Fry 1992, 174)

If this is indeed the case, much then still hangs on the question: was there really a danger of revolution? "With the benefit of hindsight we can, or course, argue that there was not" (O'Gorman 1989, 33–34).

This might be an oversimplification, lurching towards a view that ignores, as Clive Emsley asserts, British sensitivity to the concept of liberty (Emsley 1985, 801–825). It is ludicrous to suggest that the various revolutionary societies and reformist groups such as the LCS or Friends of the People did not pose some slight risk to national security and stability, yet it is equally erroneous to position the whole of Britain on the brink of open rebellion during the 1790s. The repression during Pitt's "Reign of Terror" was no new departure; it did, however, heighten the awareness of personal freedoms and, in the event, appeal to an innate sense of loyalism and self-preservation. Loyalists might view the so-called repression as a temporary inconvenience, whereas those nonconformists who found their political leanings outside the accepted norm came under suspicion and thus suffered under the "terror." Emsley is correct, then, when he argues that notwithstanding acts of terror employed by the government, such as beatings, arbitrary arrests, transportations, and indefinite gaol sentences, the legislation was a manifestation of fear designed to "preserve English liberty from a terrifying, atheistical, levelling power across the Channel and its many supporters in the United Kingdom" (2000, 2).

What is perhaps most important to our discussion is the efficacy of the measures implemented by the government to avert revolution in Britain, more especially as they pertain to the freemasons. McElroy and Peter Clark each raise interesting points in their respective studies of clubs, societies, and freemasons, with both coming to similar conclusions. McElroy notes that "not until the end of the century did social clubs seek their own buildings, and even then some of their arrangements seem strange to an age in which conviviality in the old style [was] dead" (McElroy 1969, 144). Clark echoes this argument, particularly emphasizing the role of the Secret Societies Act:

By 1800 ... there were signs that freemasonry was becoming less open ... There was a growing trend towards local lodges renting or building dedicated premises, instead of gathering in public drinking houses. Government action against seditious societies led to the [Secret] Societies Act in 1799 ... By then the formative age of freemasonry was surely over. (Clark 2000, 349)

The demise of the formative age of freemasonry is a direct consequence of the government's reaction toward seditious clubs and societies, and the ramifications for freemasons were huge. Government ministers convinced themselves of an imminent threat and imposed various pieces of legislation that were, as Harry Dickinson writes, "serious infringements of civil liberties" (Dickinson 1985, 41).

Organizations inevitably discovered means to circumvent the legislation, and those who chose to act in accordance with the law forfeited rights, privileges, and powers, in large measure to preserve their relationship with the government and safeguard themselves against undue persecution. Although Pitt's government was intent on limiting the influence of radical groups through a formidable array of repressive legislation, the "irony of these policies is that they helped to create the very problem that they were designed to solve" (Prescott 2000, 17). Indeed, the legislation forced radical organizations underground.

Andrew Prescott ironically argues that the Secret Societies Act was largely "an exercise in closing stable doors after horses had fled" (10–12). The radical societies that the government attempted to suppress continued to meet, and the societies who fell outside the scope of the Act from the onset were placed under extreme pressure to comply, such as the freemasons. As we have seen, repressive legislation was often ineffective or rarely implemented, and although it did succeed to a certain degree in checking the ostensible threat of rebellion, the government's determination to eradicate seditious and treasonable organizations caused serious masonic turmoil during the early years of the nineteenth century. Once again, allegations of involvement in the dissemination of revolutionary ideas resurfaced, triggering fresh fears of masonic ambitions to subvert the establishment. Although the masons categorically denied the veracity of such claims and affirmed their allegiance to preserving the stability of the government, internal political turmoil threatened to erode the public image so carefully crafted by the eighteenth-century freemasons.

CITED WORKS

Aberdeen Masonic Lodge No. 1(3). 1725–1810. *Aberdeen Lodge No. 1(3) Minute Books.* Aberdeen.

Ancient Grand Lodge of England. 1786–1810. *Ancient Grand Lodge of England Minute Books.* London.

Anderson, James. 1976. *The Constitutions of the Freemasons, Facsimile Edition.* London: Bernard Quaritch, Ltd.

Barrell, John. 2000. *Imagining The King's Death: Figurative Treason, Fantasies of Regicide 1793–1796.* Oxford: University Press.

Barruel, Abbe. 1798. *Memoirs, Illustrating the History of Jacobinism.* London: T. Burton and Co. No. 11, Gate Street, Lincoln's-Inn Fields, and sold by E. Booker, No. 56, New Bond-Street.

Black, Jeremy. 1999. *Eighteenth-Century Europe.* London: Palgrave Macmillan.

Brims, John. 1993. "Scottish Radicalism and the United Irishmen." In *The United Irishmen: Republicanism, Radicalism and Rebellion,* eds. Daire Keogh, David Dickson, and Kevin Whelan. Dublin: Lilliput Pr Ltd.

Clark, Peter. 2000. *British Clubs and Societies 1580–1800: The Origins of an Associational World.* Oxford: University Press.

Clifford, Robert. 1798. *Application of Barruel's Memoirs of Jacobinism to the Secret Societies of Ireland and Great Britain.* London: Sold by E. Booker.

Cochin, Augustin. 1981. "The Theory of Jacobinism." In *Interpreting the French Revolution,* ed. Francois Furet. Cambridge: University Press.

Dickinson, H. T. 1985. *British Radicalism and the French Revolution, 1789–1815.* Oxford: Blackwell Publishing.

Dilworth, Mark. 1958. "Two necrologies of Scottish Benedictine Abbey's in Germany." *IR* 9: 191.

Duffy, Michael. 2000. *Pitt The Younger.* Essex: Routledge.

Emerson, Roger. 1973. "The Enlightenment and Social Structures." In *City and Society in the 18th Century,* eds. Paul Fritz and David Williams. Toronto: Hakkert.

Emerson, Roger. 2003. "The Contexts of the Scottish Enlightenment." In *The Cambridge Companion to the Scottish Enlightenment*, ed. Alexander Broadie. Cambridge: University Press.

Emsley, Clive. 1985. "Repression, 'terror' and the rule of law in England during the decade of the French Revolution." *English Historical Review* CCCXCVII: 801–825.

Emsley, Clive. 2000. *Britain and the French Revolution*. London: Routledge.

Ferguson, William. 1965. *Scotland, 1689 to the Present: The Edinburgh History of Scotland Volume 4*. Edinburgh: Mercat Press.

Firminger, W. K. 1937. "The Romances of Robison and Barruel." *Ars Quatuor Coronatorum 50: 31–69*.

Fry, Michael. 1992. *The Dundas Despotism*. Edinburgh: University Press.

Gallin, Richard G. 1979. "Scottish Radicalism, 1792–1794." Unpublished PhD Thesis. Columbia University.

Grand Lodge of Scotland. 1736–1799. *Chartulary and List of Lodges and Members: 1736–1799*. Edinburgh.

Grand Lodge of Scotland. 1736–1765. *Grand Lodge of Scotland Minute Books Vol. I, 1736–1765*. Edinburgh.

Grand Lodge of Scotland. 1765–1795. *Grand Lodge of Scotland Minute Books Vol. II, 1765–1795*. Edinburgh.

Grand Lodge of Scotland. 1795–1810. *Grand Lodge of Scotland Minute books Vol. III, 1795–1810*. Edinburgh.

Jacob, Margaret C. 1991. *Living the Enlightenment: Freemasonry and Politics in Eighteenth-Century Europe*. Oxford: University Press.

Journeymen Masonic Lodge No. 8. 1707–1810. *Journeymen Masonic Lodge No. 8 Minute Books*. Edinburgh.

Kennedy, Michael L. 1982. *The Jacobin Clubs in the French Revolution: The First Years*. Princeton: University Press.

Lambert, Shelia (ed.). 1975. *House of Commons Sessional Papers of the Eighteenth-Century*. Wilmington: Scholarly Resources.

Lindsay, Robert Strathern. 1935. *A History of the Mason Lodge of Holyrood House (St Luke's) No. 44*. Edinburgh: T. & A. Constable.

Lynch, Michael. 2000. *Scotland: A New History*. London: Pimlico.

McElroy, David D. 1969. *Scotland's Age of Improvement: A Survey of Eighteenth-Century Literary Clubs and Societies*. Washington State: University Press.

McFarland, E. W. 1994. *Ireland and Scotland in the Age of Revolution*. Edinburgh: University Press.

Melton, James Van Horn. 2001. *The Rise of the Public in Enlightenment Europe*. Cambridge: University Press.

Money, John. 1990. "Freemasonry and the Fabric of Loyalism in Hanoverian England." In *The Transformation of Political Culture: England and Germany in the Late Eighteenth Century*, ed. Eckhart Hellmuth. Oxford: University Press.

Munck, Thomas. 2000. *The Enlightenment: A Comparative Social History 1721–1794*. London: Bloomsbury.

O'Gorman, Frank. 1989. "Pitt and the 'Tory' Reaction to the French Revolution 1789–1815." In *Britain and the French Revolution 1789-1815*, ed. H. T. Dickinson. London: Palgrave Macmillan.

Prescott, Andrew. 2000. "The Unlawful Societies Act of 1799." Conference Paper, London: Canonbury Masonic Research Centre.

Robertson, James. Personal Letter, Laing MSS II 1769 – 177. Reprinted with the permission of the University of Edinburgh Library.

Robison, John. Personal Letter, Laing MSS II 500. Reprinted with the permission of the University of Edinburgh Library.

Robison, John. 1797. *Proofs of a Conspiracy Against All the Religions and Governments of Europe, Carried on in the Secret Meetings of the Freemasons, Illuminati, and Reading Societies, Collected from Good Authorities*. Edinburgh.

Seggie, J. Stewart. 1930. *Annals of the Lodge of Journeymen Masons No. 8*. Edinburgh: Thomas Allan & Sons.

Stevenson, David. 1988. *The Origins of Freemasonry: Scotland's Century 1590–1710*. Cambridge: University Press.

Stevenson, John. 1989. "Popular Radicalism and Popular Protest." In *Britain and the French Revolution 1789–1815*, ed. H. T. Dickinson. London: Palgrave Macmillan.

St Mungo's Lodge. 1767–1810. *St Mungo's Lodge No. 27 Minute Books*. Glasgow.

Wells, Roger. 1983. *Insurrection: The British Experience 1795–1803*. Gloucester: A. Sutton.

Worts, F. R. 1965. "The Development of the Content of Masonry During the Eighteenth Century." *Ars Quatuor Coronatorum* 78: 1.

CHAPTER 2

THE STOLEN GENERATIONS IN THE AUSTRALIAN NORTHERN TERRITORY (CA 1910–CA 1970): ORIGINS SEALED IN SECRECY

Gwenaelle Hamel
University Paris-Dauphine

> We may go home, but we cannot relive our childhoods. We may reunite with our mothers, fathers, sisters, brothers, aunties, uncles, communities, but we cannot relive the twenty, thirty, forty years that we spent without their love and care, and they cannot undo the grief and mourning they felt when we were separated from them. We can go home to ourselves as Aboriginals, but this does not erase the attacks inflicted on our hearts, minds, bodies and souls, by caretakers who thought their mission was to eliminate us as Aboriginals. (Human Rights and Equal Opportunity Commission 1997, 29)[1]

This testimony of a member of the Stolen Generations sums up all the pain, grief, suffering, mistreatments, and spoliation undergone all throughout long years of separation. The victims of these forced removals from their natural families experienced these removals as real abductions, although they were legally carried out (under the successive laws ranging from the late nineteenth century to roughly the early 1970s) on the entire Australian continent. The removals were rarely ever followed by a family or even a tribal reunion. Consequently, the deep psychological suffering induced by these abductions all too often carried on under duress and a legacy that was still vivid. They firstly affected the children who were removed but also their parents who had to suffer the consequences of this loss. In the Aboriginal system of belief and kinship, these removals were perceived as a kind of social death. Consequently, they powerlessly witnessed the collapsing of a whole complex tribal system based on kinship and the destruction of a whole section of the Dreamtime.

---

1   Human Rights and Equal Opportunity Commission, *Bringing them Home* (Australia: 1997), 689.

Coined and used for the first time by the Australian historian Peter Read in *The Stolen Generations. The Removal of Aboriginal Children in New South Wales 1883–1969*, these heavily meaningful words, Stolen Generations, were chosen to designate the victims of the arbitrary removals which, as we mentioned earlier, although legally carried out were made on a racial basis against thousands of children of mixed descent who were often referred to as half-castes. Such removals were made possible under the successive policies of the different governments: policies mainly of protection, segregation, and assimilation. Throughout the years, the words Stolen Generations have become the symbol of a whole page of Australian history and a constant reminder of the assimilation policy and its failures and flaws. The Australian scholar, Robert Manne, gives a very precise and sharp definition of the concept hidden behind the term:

> Invented by the historian Peter Read, 'stolen generations' is the term that the Aboriginal people have embraced for their collective tragedy—the separation of thousands of children of mixed descent from their mothers and communities. (Manne 2001, 2)[2]

These forced removals took place all over the country, in every State and Territory, but here we will focus solely on the Northern Territory because it constitutes a special case for several reasons. First and foremost, it is a unique case due to its political status at the time. The Northern Territory did not have an independent government and depended on the decisions made by the Commonwealth Government back in Canberra. Along with the Australian Capital Territory (ACT), the Northern Territory (NT) was the only one in the country to be under the direct and unique jurisdiction of the Commonwealth Government. In other words, it was under federal responsibility. So, in a way it was used by those in power as a form of laboratory where legislative as well as social or sociobiological experiments could be made.

The Northern Territory was also chosen because of its substantial Aboriginal population concentration: although the absolute size of the Aboriginal population is less than in other states, it counts a larger share of the percentage of the total population. Indeed, according to the 2000 census, the Northern Territory had 202,729 inhabitants, among them 50,785 indigenous Australians, equivalent to 25.1% of the whole population. For com-

---

2   Robert Manne, *In Denial. The Stolen Generations and the Right* (Melbourne: Black Inc., 2001), 113.

parison, during this very same census the Aborigines represented 2.2% of the whole Australian population with 410,003 individuals. As a reminder, the estimations of the Aboriginal population at the time of colonization in 1788 vary according to anthropological studies: 300,000–1,000,000.

The socio-economic context also justifies the case study of the Northern Territory: for instance, the in-depth works launched in the Territory in order to exploit it. A perfect illustration of this would be the works that started in 1870 and lasted 2 years to complete in order to lay the line of the Overland Telegraph. Then, in 1878, the railway linking the south of the country to the north, from Adelaide (South Australia) to Darwin (Northern Territory) going through Alice Springs (Northern Territory) was launched. The living conditions in the Territory were considered to be too rough and harsh for ladies, so the workers were forbidden from bringing along their wives. Ultimately, this situation resulted in a substantial increase in the number of mixed-descent children births. Alec Ross, an Aboriginal of mixed descent and a member of the Stolen Generations, confirmed this fact during an interview with the author in 2007, stating: "no wonder so many of us were born."

More generally, the context of the time gave so little room on the social ladder to the black population and advocated white supremacy and thus explains the policies put in place. Contemporary schools of thought were decisive in the way the laws aimed at the Aborigines were adopted and applied across the Territory. The theory of Social Darwinism played a leading role in the judgments formulated by white Australians toward the natives. Herbert Spencer (1820–1903) is the father of this nineteenth-century theory, claiming that Charles Darwin's Theory of Evolution could be applied to human societies. This provided the Australians with a possible alibi. They had thus discovered a justification for the social and biological selection they put in place by attempting to eliminate the weakest members of their society through the implementation of a system that was very similar to eugenics. In other words, they had just found a pseudo-scientific justification for the acts they were committing against the first inhabitants of the land.

In 1911, the Commonwealth Government took the lead of the Northern Territory following South Australia's governance (1863–1911) and was then confronted with the new face of what was then called the "Aboriginal problem," the face of these thousands of children who were mostly born from the forced union between an Aboriginal woman and a white male. For the Government, time and money should no longer be spent on full-blood Aborigines. They were then considered as a doomed race, but on these half-castes or children of mixed descent of whom it intended to take care, wishing to protect them from the negative influence supposedly induced by their black blood and culture, and put the emphasis on their white heritage to promote the unique image of a White Australia tainted of Western values.

The Government, scared of being rapidly outnumbered, decided that it had to put an end to this situation. The only solution it could envision was to stop or at least slow down the rapid spread of births. The different steps to achieve this attempt at controlling the number of births were executed within a judicial and legislative framework. All the Aboriginal Ordinances voted from 1911 on in the Northern Territory had only one alleged goal that people could easily perceive as being worthwhile: saving the mixed descent children. The only problem was that the consequences of their implementation were far from the expected results. In the mind of the authorities, as well as of the different Chief Protectors of the Aborigines, the only suitable and viable solution to the situation was to control every single aspect and detail of the life of the Aborigines regardless of the cost and the means. However, this generated a great deal of dramatic consequences. These included a brutal and definite break from their aboriginality following the removal from their families, their clans, and their very unique and particular vision of the world around them. It is hard for people educated in the West to apprehend all the implications of belonging to a tribe or an Aboriginal family in the wider sense of the term. The kinship system defines the rights to land, marriages, and taboos about the relationships between the members of a same tribe or even within a single family. By cutting these links, a whole section of the tribal and family story disappears. The other devastating consequences include giving up their birth name, the absence of contact with their families, evangelization, and periods of residence of varying length in missions or in foster families to be given an education, and their exploitation in minor jobs such as servants or maids without any financial compensation. They were trained for farm jobs in order to build up a cheap and malleable workforce that could easily be exploited.

The Aboriginal Ordinance 1911 and those that followed authorized the Chief Protector of the Aborigines to "take in custody" any children whom he considered as being neglected or in danger. The simple fact of belonging to an Aboriginal family meant for the authorities that there was some kind of neglect. When the children were taken away from their families, they were then sent to missions or government-run institutions. In the Northern Territory, the most infamous ones were the Bungalow in Alice Springs and the Kahlin Compound in Darwin.

The Aboriginal Ordinances set up a whole system of categories depending on how much white blood the children had in them. There was a whole list of denominations: mixed blood, quadroon, and octoroon among others. A selective sorting of human beings was put in place, according to the amount of white blood flowing in the veins of the children. This was done in the hope of creating an elite of children of mixed descent that would then be able to marry white people over time and so have a child with fairer skin that would marry a white person and have a child with a fairer and fairer skin and so on until all outward signs of Aboriginal ancestry disappeared. From 1927, this was the policy of absorption advocated by Dr. Cecil Cook, the Northern Territory Chief Protector of the Aborigines. He was a strong advocate of the "breed the colour out" doctrine. A.O. Neville[3] was also a strong advocate of this doctrine in Western Australia. He achieved part of his plan through marriage control. An Aboriginal woman willing to marry a white male had to fill in a specific application to the Protector and then it was decided whether to grant a marriage permit. This was nothing but an undisguised attempt to try and make them fit in a white mould, deny them a personal choice, and consider them as being irresponsible people, unable to handle their own lives.

Barbara Cummings, who is one of the founders of *Karu*,[4] an association working for family reunions, is also a victim of the Stolen Generations. She is a former resident of the Darwin Kahlin Compound and the Retta Dixon Home, two institutions for children of mixed descent. In *Take this Child ... From Kahlin Compound to the Retta Dixon Children's Home*,[5] she writes about the constant abuse, the lies, and the acts of mistreatment and deprivation that the inmates suffered on a daily basis. They experienced deprivation and humiliation because of the color of their skin, their beliefs, or even

---

3   Auber Octavius Neville (1875–1954), a Chief Protector of the Aborigines in Western Australia from 1915 to 1940.

4   Karu means child in Gurindji, an Aboriginal traditional language.

5   Barbara Cummings, *Take this Child ... From Kahlin Compound to the Retta Dixon Children's Home* (Canberra: Aboriginal Studies Press for the Australian Institute of Aboriginal and Torres Strait Islander Studies, 1990), 139.

their languages—in a word because of their differences. Every single thing that constituted their aboriginality was systematically taken away from them, hidden, left untold, or openly denigrated. For example, they could not communicate in their own traditional language—they had to abandon it for the English language. Numerous members of the Stolen Generations testified that after being caught speaking their dialect, they had their mouth washed with soap in an attempt to clean them from the stain of aboriginality. A new identity was then imposed upon them without letting them have the slightest choice of whether to adopt or reject it, an identity somehow injected into them under duress and violence but also involving daily and recurring belittlement.

The weight of secrecy about their origins was a constant burden they had to bear. In order to keep a slight bond with their culture they had to do it in secret so as not to succumb to the scolding of the Home employees. They also had to put up with the lies of those so-called carers, some of whom went so far as to tell the children that their parents were deceased or that they had abandoned them. Most of the time the parents were not offered any options. Or they were forced to sign papers that they could barely read but that they wrongly saw as the guarantee of a brighter future, the Open Sesame to an egalitarian society, without understanding the dramatic sacrifices and consequences they would actually generate.

It is important to bear in mind that missionaries also played an important part at this period of time. Their goal was to impose a new religion on the children, a religion that was totally alien to them, having nothing in common with their beliefs, forcing them to integrate new and abstract notions. When it comes to the subject of the spirituality of the Aboriginal people, one must mention the Dreamtime, their creation time, a time belonging only to them. For the Australian anthropologist Ronald Berndt: "Everything associated with the Dreaming—and it is hard to find anything that is not—is religious. The Dreaming embraced virtually every aspect of Aboriginal activity." (Ronald Berndt, *Aboriginal Australian Art*, 117)

Coined at the end of the nineteenth century by Spencer and Gillen after their study of the Arrernte tribe in Central Australia, the English term Dreamtime is the translation of the word *"alchera."*

The cosmology of the Dreamtime is a concept that is hard to apprehend for Westerners, as it is integrated in the daily life of the different tribes spread all over the country. According to Barbara Glowczewski, a French anthropologist, "The Dreamtime or Dreaming is a space-time parallel to human temporality and with which life on earth maintains a feedback relationship" (Glowczewski 1991, 16).[6] In other words, it is a flux in perpetual temporal evolution that does not refer to any static or fixed period of time. It encompasses all the concepts of time and space: the beginning, a time of creation, the power contained in the different places where the Creative Spirits went to when they created them, and the power of the things that they have touched and that consequently share the same essence as them. The behavior of the Aborigines is ruled by this creative past and by the homage they have to pay to the Spirits. In Aboriginal belief, the Creative Spirits awoke from a very long sleep and began their wanderings on Earth and created all the living features of the land. For them, these spirits are the creators of all living or non-living things and that is why they have to be brought to life again on a regular basis through the different rites and ceremonies.

Essentially, the past, the present, and the future are all interrelated and all derive from one another. This means that the past is still very much alive in the present and the future. Today's types of behaviors were already implicitly contained in the past. We may sum it up in a way that may seem paradoxical to many: "yesterday will be and tomorrow was." When the members of the Stolen Generations were deprived of this special relationship and the bond with their land, Dreamings, rites and myths they lost their spiritual contact and connection with their origins and so were no more a part of this natural world with which they used to live in perfect harmony. Indeed, for the Aborigines, land is not perceived in a materialistic perspective but in a spiritual one, a vision that runs counter to the one held by the newcomers and the two seem even today quite irreconcilable with one another.

Besides having to adopt a new religion and a new language, being cut off from their origins also meant that they had to adapt to something that may seem trivial but which represented real suffering for them. They were used to leading a nomadic life, as hunter-gatherers, and all of a sudden they had to wear clothes and settle down. For some of these children, just the fact that they wore shoes was close to torture, they pictured it as a costume they had to wear to look like white children. Their inside was washed with soap

---

6   Glowczewski, Barbara, *Du rêve à la loi chez les Aborigènes* (Paris: Presses Universitaires de France, 1991), 362. "Le Dreamtime ou Dreaming est un espace-temps parallèle à la temporalité humaine et avec lequel la vie sur terre entretient une relation de feedback."

as mentioned before and their outside was also modified so that they were disguised to project the image of perfectly assimilated children.

Some of these children were resilient and managed to find their own place in society, but for the great majority of them, the damages were irreparable: the impossibility and inability to find their way either into the white society that rejected them or into the Aboriginal society that no longer recognized them since they had been deprived of the social codes that govern the tribes. Sometimes the impossibility of communication also made this rejection possible.

Alec Ross, who is known around Alice Springs as the legend of the Telegraph Station, considers that it was an opportunity for him to be removed from his mother and that being raised in governmental institutions was a real chance—a chance for survival. The Telegraph Station known today as a tourist attraction was an institution for children of mixed descent at the beginning of the twentieth century known as the Bungalow. The children who were sent to the Bungalow received only minimal education because the curriculum was different for white and mixed-descent children. People held the view that the Aboriginal children were unable to learn or be educated up to the same standard as their white fellows. This view was to some extent supported by tests conducted by Stanley David Porteus[7] among the Aboriginal mission population in the twentieth century using the Porteus Maze test.[8]

The members of the Stolen Generations were—and still are today for those who are still alive—caught in between two worlds, stuck in limbo from which it is hard to escape. It is as if they were cut in two halves: a black body trying to find its balance standing on a white leg and a black leg; the problem being that those in power are trying to cut this black leg off. They are the product of two cultures that are in conflict. On the one hand, the mainstream culture that promised them that they would belong ends up rejecting them, and, on the other hand, cosmology is lost, belonging to the Dreamtime is broken and a whole section of it thus disappears. From this perspective, it is unthinkable not to mention the intergenerational effects of this trauma linked to the tearing apart of a natural family. The testimonies of the victims show a real incapacity to share bonds of love with their own children or with their natural families when they are re-united with them.

---

7   Stanley David Porteus (1883–1972), Australian psychologist, educationist and writer.

8   Non-verbal test of intelligence.

The Stolen Generations also suffered the psychological effects induced by trauma experienced over many years—loneliness, depression, or anguish to name a few.

Not only were the origins kept secret, they were also destroyed. Some associations such as Link-Up which try to locate and look for the natural families of the victims allow them to find some kind of equilibrium, a part of themselves that has been denied for so long and buried deep down—a feeling of pride in their retrieved aboriginality. The Stolen Generations can now try and stand with pride. The Aboriginal author Sally Morgan perfectly illustrates the ideas of secrets and secrecy in her novel *My Place*.[9] In the book, she mentions her childhood memories. She refers to the seal of secrecy imposed by her family concerning their Aboriginal ancestry. She grew up surrounded by lies that were sustained for years by her grandmother, as well as her mother who kept telling her that they had Indian origins, until there came the shock of a revelation when a whole life based on lies collapsed. She then had to go on a quest for her identity. For Sally Morgan, there was the feeling of belonging to a community that collapses, after which another one had to be found.

The lie was passed on from generation to generation because of the shame felt by a part of the Aboriginal community. The missionaries, the Protectors of the Aborigines, and the matrons of the Homes so desperately attempted to reinforce the shame through daily humiliations, so that the Aborigines would end up being ashamed of their origins and then reject other members of the Aboriginal community, including their parents or families, for those who managed to stay in touch despite the risk incurred.

The ultimate goal, from the second half of the twentieth century, at the peak of the removals designed to institutionalise the children, seemed to have been to make them "useful" citizens. To be "useful" meant that they had to be active citizens in the economic system and not dependent on it. According to the Australian anthropologist Charles Dunford Rowley (1906–1985), "as far as possible the policy was to prevent them being conceived; and to give to those who were special tuition as children, in institutions, since their white blood offered hope that they would make useful citizens" (Rowley 1970, 236).[10]

---

9   Sally Morgan, *My Place* (Western Australia: Fremantle Arts Centre Press, 1988), 349.

10 C. D. Rowley, *The Destruction of Aboriginal Society* (Hong Kong: Pelican Books, 1986 with note to preface (1970)), 430.

However, the opposite happened: the system that was put in place along with its package of laws only excluded them even more from mainstream society, marginalizing and stigmatizing them. One can wonder how and why the final result was so far from the hopes and good intentions at the outset. Taking into account the political and cultural context of the time, we can wonder if it was really going to be possible to integrate smoothly the different worlds of white and black individuals, especially in the context of a settlement.

The question of the loss of identity through institutionalization is linked to many other subjects such as land rights, self-determination, and the concept of national Reconciliation. The Reconciliation process is the consequence and the outcome of this part of Australian-Aboriginal history. The study of this history cannot be set apart from the political and social context of the time, nor studied out of the current context. This question cannot be treated in isolation; it has to be put into perspective. It is quite difficult not only to judge these past acts according to our modern criteria, values, morals, and mentality, but also to assess them keeping in mind the reality of the time. Learning from the past seems to be a pre-condition for not committing the same mistakes all over again, thereby improving the living conditions for all. Walking along the long road of collective healing can only be done with some kind of recognition of mistakes and mistreatments in order to live with this past, freed from shame or guilt, hoping to face a future not only in the context of a reconciliation process but also one of recognition of otherness and mutual acceptance.

One of the main targets of current and past governments is to fight the social and identity crisis that is deep-rooted in Australian society. The Aborigines represent the most disadvantaged socio-economic class in the country, with a life expectancy of 25 years less than the rest of the population. This fact can be explained by a high poverty rate, a high unemployment rate, and a lack of access to education, among other factors.

The social situation has slowly but surely evolved and improved since the 1960s. This decade was a turning point for the Aborigines who then tried to win back their identity. For instance, the Freedom Ride organized in 1965 by Charles Perkins, himself a member of the Stolen Generations, played an important role in the decision to hold a referendum in 1967 that concerned two sections of the Australian Constitution regarding the Aborigines. Australian voters had to decide whether the Aborigines should be included in the census and whether the Commonwealth Government should be allowed to make special laws for them. The victory was a real landslide, with 90.77% in favor of the yes option. The turning point for the Stolen Generations happened 28 years later in 1995 when the *Bringing them Home*[11] Report was released by the Human Rights and Equal Opportunity Commission. The report contains testimonies from many of the protagonists of the times, analysis of different laws implemented at the time and, more importantly, recommendations designed to help and support the victims.

With the aim of recovery and a feeling of pride in their origins, the Australian Aborigines made good use of their art to try and transmit a message to the world. What is today called Aboriginal art was thus named by Western people with their personal cultural criteria as well as their own values. For the Aborigines, it is not about art but about visually codified expressions of their beliefs, rites, myths, and an updating of past (but still active) events belonging to the peculiar world of the Dreamtime. These themes are inherent in their works of art and are for this reason connected to the sacred. For the Aborigines, there is no real aesthetic theorization in their artistic expression. The art label imposed by Westerners rests not only on a misunderstanding but also on a faulty interpretation of this hardly classifiable production.

In the Aboriginal view, only the initiated person has the right to create, to look at, or interpret these works of art. It is forbidden by traditional law to give away such secrets to profane eyes. This is at the heart of the issue concerning aboriginal art today, since it has to be modified before being sold to people who are ignorant of the power of some symbols. This is a way for Aboriginal people to open the door slightly to the Dreamtime but without letting anybody in at the same time. Their goal seems to be to help white people find their way to their traditional culture by only showing some parts of it through an educational process.

Some will only see a succession of dots, lines, or sketches drawn without any logical approach other than the instant fantasy of the artist and assembled, while some others will see a map, some kind of representation of the Australian continent as it is seen and felt by its first inhabitants. As Jean-

---

11 Human Rights and Equal Opportunity Commission. *Bringing them Home, National Inquiry into the Separation of Aboriginal and Torres Strait Islander Children from Their Families* (Australia: 1997), 689.

Pierre Barou wrote, "the eye thinks (*L'oeil pense*)"[12] but no longer thinks the same things when it is initiated.

As mentioned earlier, since the early 1960s, the claims of the Aborigines regarding the acknowledgment of their rights and the granting of citizenship have been asserted. Art has played a great role in this struggle for recognition and some Aboriginal artists have played an important role through their pieces. They were symbolically used as banners, with the difference that the paintings also apparently have a more significant impact since they are meant to last and be desired, purchased, and then exhibited and therefore be seen by the largest number and therefore raise public awareness over time.

It is quite obvious that the question of the Stolen Generations and their lost identity is still vivid in the twenty-first century undeniable progress. In the Northern Territory, this very special place, with its significant concentration of Aboriginal population, one can still feel today the devastating and enduring impact of the different policies toward the Aborigines throughout the last century.

How can it be possible to recover after being snatched from your family, roots, and everything that constitutes your inner identity such as values and customs? This is a question the Aborigines had to answer both for themselves and sometimes for the luckiest ones with their new-found family or community. Australia is a country that is today longing for an ever-growing role on the world stage and particularly in Oceania, and it cannot afford to exclude a whole portion of its population. Therefore, it seems that in order to become an egalitarian society, Australian people have to re-invent their relationship with the natives of the country and this means changing their vision of them. On the Aboriginal side, it also seems necessary for them to look for an alternative attitude that sometimes resembles victimization, which is preventing them from moving forward.

Despite this position, it seems necessary, not to say essential, to abandon once and for all the expression that has been used so often as a justification of the different policies put in place towards the Aborigines, "for their own good,"[13] in favor of "for our own good," meaning the good of the white Aus-

---

12 Jean-Pierre Barou, *L'œil pense. Essai sur les arts primitifs* (Paris: Editions Payot et Rivages, 2002), 224.

13 Anna Haebich, *For their own Good. Aborigines and Government in the South West of*

tralians who felt threatened by the spread of the mixed-descent children, pictured as a danger to the White Australia that was so much desired by politicians and settlers.

It is quite clear that the issue of the Stolen Generations encompasses all aspects of Australian society, particularly the political and socio-economic positions. Today's situation is nothing but the reflection of past actions and decisions made at a time when they seemed adequate and appropriate. The problem goes beyond the sole question of the Stolen Generations; it concerns the entire Aboriginal community.

Indeed, numerous voices rose from the different social strata to try to go against what seemed inhumane in many people's eyes, but they were not strong or numerous enough to be heard in the dominant flow of the time. The weight of education and society was too overwhelming. It took more than two centuries for Australia to publicly recognize the past mistakes against its indigenous population. The road to Reconciliation seems to have come to an end with the historical speech given by the former Labour Prime Minister Kevin Rudd on February 13, 2008. The apology given on behalf of the whole nation to apologize for the past mistreatments, more particularly to the victims of the Stolen Generations[14], seems to be a stepping-stone for real change.

There is still one question that seems to remain unanswered: are we witnessing, as a passive and powerless audience, the disappearance and disintegration of the oldest continuing living culture on the planet? Today, the Aborigines are no longer fighting for their survival from a biological and human point of view, but they are fighting for recognition, recognition being a form of cultural survival. Despite the crumbling foundations of their society, culture, and system of values and beliefs, the Aborigines have survived and still live today in a world that continues to close its doors in their faces. One can wonder if we are not now facing a lost culture rather than a stolen generation.

Hope remains strong for the Aborigines to be accepted in a genuine and profound way. This hope may be as simple as what Harold Furber, a stolen

---

Western Australia 1900–1940 (Western Australia: 1998), 413.

14 Kevin Rudd: "We apologise especially for the removal of Aboriginal and Torres Strait Islander children from their families, their communities and their country. For the pain, suffering and hurt of these Stolen Generations, their descendants and for their families left behind, we say sorry. To the mothers and the fathers, the brothers and the sisters, for the breaking up of families and communities, we say sorry".

child, once told the author: "they should stop to consider us as the problem but as the solution."

BIBLIOGRAPHY

Barou, Jean-Pierre. 2002. *L'oeil pense*. France: Petite Bibliothèque Payot.

Cummings, Barbara. 1990. *Take this Child ... From Kahlin Compound to the Retta Dixon Children's Home*. Canberra: Aboriginal Studies Press for the Australian Institute of Aboriginal and Torres Strait Islander Studies.

Glowczewski, Barbara. 1991. *Du rêve à la loi chez les Aborigènes*. Paris: Presses Universitaires de France.

Haebich, Anna. *For their own Good. Aborigines and Government in the South West of Western Australia 1900–1940*. Western Australia, 1998 Second Edition (1988, 1989, 1992).

Human Rights and Equal Opportunity Commission. 1997. *Bringing them Home. National Inquiry into the Separation of Aboriginal and Torres Strait Islander Children from Their Families*. Australia: Commonwealth of Australia.

Manne, Robert. 2001. *In Denial. The Stolen Generation and the Right*. Melbourne: Black, Inc.

Morgan, Sally. 1988 (1987). *My Place*. Western Australia: Fremantle Arts Centre Press.

Rowley, C. D. *The Destruction of Aboriginal Society*. Hong Kong: Pelican Books, 1986 with note to preface 1970.

CHAPTER 3

"A LOCAL DIFFICULTY"?
ENOCH POWELL'S SECRET MOTIVATIONS
TO RESIGN FROM THE TREASURY
IN 1958 AND ITS AFTERMATH

Stéphane Porion
University François Rabelais, Tours

The year at the Treasury was a very important year. The year in which three politicians, almost in isolation from the theories of the civil service found themselves obliged to address their minds to the question of inflation, its causes and its remedy, and came up, although very different personalities and dealing with very different subject matter, with what was essentially the same answer. And I suppose the development of that answer which has come to be known as monetarism has occupied my mind and my speeches ever since in the last thirty years. (...) Certainly that was an important formative year, and it was a year from which lines of force ran out through the rest of my political life. (Shepherd 1997, 152)

A large number of British people only recall Prime Minister Harold Macmillan's emphasis on prosperity to the detriment of his warning against inflation in his July 20, 1957 "never-had-it-so-good" speech:

Let's be frank about it; most of our people have never had it so good. Go around the country, go to the industrial towns, go to the farms, and you will see a state of prosperity such as we have never had in my lifetime—nor indeed ever in the history of this country. (Macmillan 1971, 350)

Furthermore, *The Daily Mail* wrote in Macmillan's December 1986 necrologies that "Macmilllan—Supermac, Super Statesman—had brought Great Britain years of prosperity, peace and progress" (Horne 1989, xiii). After the Conservative 1959 landslide victory at the General Election, Macmillan proudly depicted British society to the Queen as one indulging in unprecedented mass-consumerism and well-being (Hennessy 2006, 3). Yet, historian Peter Clarke critically stresses that Macmillan successfully managed to create and fuel his own mythical image of *"Macwonder"* throughout the late 1950s (Sampson 1967, 157) and argues:

> The bastardized message, "You've never had it so good", went down as his most famous utterance, and folk myth has him stumping the country on this slogan in the 1959 General Election. If there is a poetic truth in this, it is because Macmillan projected himself with a verve which teetered on the brink of vulgarity. (Clarke 1992, 225)

Macmillan simply aimed to apply his main economic ideas—ideas that were encompassed in *The Middle Way* he had drafted 20 years before and imbued with paternalism and economic opportunity, and to set up "the Opportunity State" (Lowe 1989, 158; PSG (57) 1; POLL 3/2/1/2). He had accounted for his economic approach in March 1958: "With good management and reasonable restraint, the possibilities of expansion without inflation are almost boundless" (Macmillan 1966, xxv). As historian Stuart Mitchell put it in 2006, Macmillan called for "Minimalist statecraft": "It was geared towards the pursuit of domestic stability and limited policy goals that would ensure the reconstruction of Tory morale and, in due course, success at the polls" (Mitchell 2006, 38). Macmillan appointed Enoch Powell and Nigel Birch as, respectively, Financial Secretary and Economic Secretary to the Treasury, with a view to trim public spending and cope with the issue of inflation. Simon Heffer, Powell's biographer, shrewdly comments upon this nomination:

> Ironically, the job realistically within his grasp that [Powell] most wanted—the post of Financial Secretary to the Treasury—was given to him by a man who, before Edward Heath assumed the mantle, would represent to Powell all that he found regrettable about the principle-free conduct of politics. (Heffer 1999, 210–211)

Powell was put in charge of establishing provisional budget spending estimates for each Department to help freshly appointed Chancellor of the Exchequer, Peter Thorneycroft, to sketch the main lines of his economic and financial policy. The former had a "Gladstonian instinct" (Jarvis 1995, 23), "giving a moralistic edge to his cost-cutting drive" (Shepherd 1997, 163).

The two Treasury Secretaries "served as the Chancellor's praetorian guard" (Jarvis 1995, 160). According to Robert Shepherd, this triumvirate comprised very different personalities from different backgrounds, who nevertheless, staunchly agreed on the same political stance: "They should take a very tough line this year and that the general doctrine should be no expansion" (Turner 1994, 227; NA, PRO T 230/408; NA, PRO T 227/485).

In the autumn of 1957, Powell's governmental budget estimates showed that provisional public expenditure was on the rise in the 1958 government budget. The Treasury triumvirate could not accept this as it would result in increasing inflation and breach their golden rule—that budget estimates should not exceed those of previous year in real terms. After a range of emergency Cabinet meetings called by the Chancellor of the Exchequer in December 1957, the Cabinet eventually dismissed the golden rule and refused a further £50m budget cut because they were not prone to cut welfare spending—which would basically mean abolishing family allowances for second children and raising both National Insurance contributions and charges for school milk. The dispute over the 1% budget cut, amounting only to £100 million, undermined the Treasury ministers' credibility to hold down inflation and preserve the position of sterling through money-supply control. They had no choice but to resign on January 6 to express their opposition to Macmillan's expansionist and Keynesian policies.

Although the Treasury triumvirate's resignation seemed to "throw fresh light on the old conflicts in economic policy, and on the behaviour of the Conservative Party" (*The Spectator* January 1, 1958, 64), Macmillan had no fear that his government would collapse and thus confidently left for a Commonwealth tour the next day (Horne 1989, 75). In John Ramsden's view, the resignations did not mean so much a clash on budget estimates, but rather an ego struggle (Ramsden 1996, 33). However, the Treasury resignation has become mythology in the history of the Conservative Party: Thorneycroft and Powell have often been compared to "prophets of monetarism" (Robbins 1990, 401; Garnett and Hickson 2009, 60; Carr and Hart 2013, 43) and his September 1957 emergency financial measures, notably the bank rate increase to 7%, to "Thatcherism and Friedmanism with a vengeance" (Pugh 1994, 248; Lamb 1995, 48). This view has been much challenged (Seldon and Ball 1994, 49) and historian E. H. H. Green argues that "to see a direct link in terms of underlying economic ideas and policy between the Treasury resignations of 1958 and developments in the 1970s and 1980s is an error. But that does not mean that there are no instructive historical parallels to be drawn" (Lowe 1989, 519–520; Green 2002, 212). At most, Thorneycroft's financial policy embodied what Powell called "a gleam in the eye of monetarism" (Peden 95–96; POLL 3/2/4/13). To fill a gap in the historiography, Chris Cooper wrote an article in 2011, which encompassed Thorneycroft's whole career to attempt to trace the origins of Thatcherism (Cooper 2011).

However, one moot point has not been solved yet: who influenced whom among the Treasury triumvirate to resign? Matthew Jarvis acknowledged that he could not make out what Powell's actual influence had been on the Chancellor (Jarvis 1995, 4). He vindicated Alistair Horne's view—based on contemporary politicians' memoirs, that Birch and Powell would have influenced Thorneycroft's economic policy and determination to resign. Edmund Bell used Macmillan's writings to uphold the same vantage point (Macmillan 1971, 372): "The ideologues, Birch and Powell, were the men really responsible for Thorneycroft's unyielding attitude" (Dell 1997, 240). Before his private papers became available to the public in 2003, Powell had always dissuaded historians from trying to shed light on the two Treasury secretaries' influence over the Chancellor: "There are no speeches or committee meetings [to be found at the Public Record Office] which are relevant to the resignations" (Jarvis 1995, 4).

Prime Minister Macmillan nonchalantly dismissed the resignations as "little local difficulties" so as to reassure international markets and British people on the Cabinet's determination to preserve the sterling and economic expansion and materialism. Macmillan skillfully covered up the truth about an ideological divide within his Cabinet over how to struggle with inflation and continue to deliver welfare provisions at the same time. He had managed to put his party in the clear from the detrimental impact of the Suez crisis by the means of efficient rhetoric on prosperity he could not abruptly put to an end because of a rigorous narrow-minded Treasury triumvirate. Moreover, "in the mind of Macmillan at least, it represented a challenge to his authority" (Jefferys 72). Therefore, this paper touches on the idea of "the art of secrecy to implement and secure power" (Horn 2006, 39), as Macmillan intended to avoid a drain on reserves which would inevitably jeopardize the pound and raise popular anxiety. The way Macmillan dealt with the Treasury resignation may not have been particularly questionable morally or legally, but his strategy to conceal the truth from the public "aimed at stabilizing a situation of imminent danger or crisis. Secrecy and the acts committed under its veil can be conceived of as such an exceptional instrument: a political measure [...] necessary for exceptional situations or goals" (Horn 2006, 41). Macmillan can be seen as "a Machiavellian leader" (Bale 2012, 89) who "regarded secrecy simply as a tool of power and it was power that legitimated." In other words, he "placed secrecy at the service of unrestrained power" (Gabis 1978, 140 and 143).

Since the Treasury resignation, Macmillan had done his utmost to win the October 1959 General Election through buying votes with prosperity promises. The Conservatives launched an efficient campaign slogan in materialistic terms: "Life's better with the Conservatives, Don't let Labour ruin it." Macmillan eventually won the elections with a landslide victory, before however being compelled to reappoint Powell in his government in 1960. However, as Kevin Jefferys notices:

> Behind the scenes, there were signs before October 1959 that ministers thought a high price was being paid for victory. Painful decisions could be shelved but not avoided indefinitely. Butler spoke in 1958 of a bleak outlook that contained seeds of troubles; [...] and Amory as Chancellor warned colleagues that commitments planned for 1960–1961 onwards would far exceed the resources likely to be available and would be liable to provoke a recurrence of the inflationary pressure which was only now being brought under control. (Jefferys 84)

The Treasury resignation has been much debated, but there have not yet been any studies to assess Powell's behind-the-scene role and motivations to resign. In addition, an analysis of the Powell papers at Churchill College, Cambridge, unveils a fresh narrative which fills some of the gaps in the historiography and also provides a critical insight of Macmillan's "never-had-it-so-good" Premiership in the late 1950s. As a matter of fact, Powell disclosed in his private correspondence that he had secret reasons to resign.

In Powell's eye, Macmillan epitomized "the old manipulative actor-manager" (Horne 1989, 153), who expected "financial rectitude" in private from his Treasury ministers (Jarvis 1995, 26) while, in public, he tried to look good by advocating the primacy of social services and economic expansion. Powell depicted Macmillan as a Machiavellian leader whose typical features were "cynicism, agnosticism, bread and circuses, European combinations, a readiness to try any wheeze (provided it helps to keep power), and a contempt for principle and politics" (Powell 1980, 18; Schofield 2013, 116). Powell staunchly challenged Macmillan's mythical representation of Supermac:

> From 1958 to 1963 one man placed upon the Conservative party and Government, and thus upon the political history of our time, his own stamp and express image, which will not for long be obliterated. The year 1958 was even statistically a turning point in so many trends in the course of events of the last fifteen years (...) It is not a coincidence that it was just in the first days of 1958 that Harold Macmillan, who had been Prime Minister for little under a year, defeated his Chancellor of the Exchequer, Peter Thorneycroft, and settled for inflation. (Hennessy 2006, 547)

In addition, Powell condemned Macmillan's manipulative stance on prosperity and his sacrifice of the Treasury triumvirate, designed to seek re-election:

> Like many phrases [such as "most of our people have never had it so good"] taken unfairly out of context, it nevertheless tells a larger truth. The conflict which six months later resulted in the unparalleled resignation of all Treasury ministers had much to do with that truth. Whether or not he really thought that Stockton in the thirties was lurking round the corner, Macmillan already aimed at winning in 1959 on public expenditure. (Powell 1980, 18)

Powell contended that Macmillan had started a crisis within his cabinet as "the First Lord of the Treasury [failed] to support the Second Lord. (...) In plain terms, the Prime Minister and the Chancellor must see eye to eye. It follows that a common understanding both of the language of public finance and of the implications of the financial policy being pursued must at all times exist between these two" (Powell 1958, 3; POLL 3/1/16). As Powell was much interested in pushing further his analysis on inflation, he started a secret correspondence with an anti-Keynesian economist in Cambridge, Denis Robertson, to support the upsides of controlling the money supply. This paper aims to unfold this new narrative by focusing on Powell's practice of secrecy, but also on his denunciation of it to avoid becoming a backbencher and to re-join the government a couple of years later as a powerful senior figure in the Conservative Party. It will also provide a critical insight into Macmillan's "never-had-it-so-good" premiership in the late 1950s, as well as of the myth of "Thatcherism *avant la lettre*."

THE TREASURY TRIUMVIRATE'S RESIGNATION IN PERSPECTIVE

Matthew Jarvis points out that Macmillan's note to his ministers on budget estimates brought to the fore the issues that would inevitably lead to a clash between Cabinet ministers and the Treasury triumvirate in December 1957 and January 1958:

> Ministers were bound by collective responsibility to accept this as their aim. However Macmillan had refined the objectives subtly by inviting reductions "whenever possible." In retrospect, this seems to have created the room for disagreement that divided the Treasury team from the rest of the Cabinet. For the Treasury ministers there seemed nothing ambiguous in Macmillan's circular; yet for spending ministers it implied a degree of elasticity in their figures. This explains the tension when it became clear that the Cabinet were not going to adhere to previous policy decisions. (Jarvis 1995, 29)

In the first place, Macmillan received a positive response from his most influential ministers, such as Lord Hailsham (NA, PRO PREM 11/2306, August 1957). However, they rapidly started expressing concerns about the Chancellor's economic policy decisions (Hall, 44). At the same time, Macmillan was undeniably influenced by Roy Harrod, one of his economic advisers, who was a fervent champion of Keynesian policies:

> The idea that you can reduce prices by limiting the quantity of money is pre-Keynesian. Keynes spent half his energy inveighing against precisely that idea. Hardly any economist under the age of 50 would subscribe to it. If it were supposed that the Conservatives were associated with such an idea, that might drive many middle of the road economists into the ranks of Labour. (...) I do sincerely hope that no Govt. speaker will use words implying that the Govt. subscribes to such an antiquated doctrine. (NA, PRO, PREM 11/2973, September 7, 1957; Green 2002, 176)

When Thorneycroft asked the Prime Minister to reaffirm his warning to the ministers in December 1957, realizing that they were "faced with the largest increase in Estimates ever recorded in peace time" (NA, PRO PREM 11/2306, December 8, 1957; Powell December 1957, 1), Macmillan cunningly qualified his instructions on December 11, 1957: "Public expenditure should be reduced, but that the reductions should not be of nature which might jeopardise the attainment of the government's long term objective of establishing wage restraint" (NA, PRO CAB 130/139; GEN 625, December 11, 1957). This gave leeway to his Cabinet ministers to block the Treasury triumvirate's financial priorities and proposals. In early January 1957, although Thorneycroft still held that the Cabinet should accept a £130m budget cut (Powell January 1958, 3), Macmillan turned out to be responsible for the final Cabinet dispute over £50m as he insidiously pushed other ministers not to back up the Chancellor's proposal:

> The Cabinet should pledge themselves to obtaining as nearly as possible the Chancellor's objective of ensuring that government expenditure in 1958–1959 did not exceed the level of 1957–1958. But it was doubtful whether the Government should hope to achieve a precise arithmetical equilibrium without injury to their other purposes. (NA, PRO CAB 128/32, January 5, 1958, 5–7)

Thornecroft and Powell thus failed to convince the Cabinet to agree on a £130m cut in welfare spending, which would have amounted to abolishing family allowances for second children or increasing hospitalization fees (Cockett 1995, 164; Shepherd 1997, 163 and 178). Macmillan argued that the budget estimates only accounted for a 1% increase compared to the previous year, which was not a burning issue at all since it supported the government's stance on preserving the pound and on delivering efficient welfare services. As for *The Economist*, it considered Macmillan's decision as a setback to Powell and Birch who held the golden rule as a whim:

> It leads to the cynical but widely heard assertion in Whitehall that second secretaries in the Treasury are currently the most powerful men in the country. The strains are particularly great when those second secretaries are working to a rigid formula; this year the Treasury formula was that government current expenditure in 1958–59 should be no higher than in 1957–58. Such a formula (...) has precious little logic to recommend it.

[It] ought to depend on the standard of social services decided upon as a long-term policy and the number of people likely to call on those social services next year. (*The Economist* January 11, 1958, 90; POLL 3/1/14)

Later, Powell reluctantly acknowledged: "Harold Macmillan was always an anti-Treasury man. (...) In the end he could shoot the pianist. However, that's the essence of a Prime Minister" (Boapah 13). Powell was accused by Macmillan's supporters, like Edward Heath, of being the mastermind of a conspiracy (Harris 2011, 426) referred to in the archives as "the Svengali theory" to bring down the Prime Minister—accusations that Powell had always refuted:

> You have to know nothing about politics to imagine that the junior ministers however clever or however influential can force a Cabinet minister after hours and days of pummelling in Cabinet finally resign. That's not within the compass of what is real practical politics. (POLL 5/35, January 1, 1989; Shepherd 1997, 164; Hennessy 2006, 545–546)

Powell also claimed that "Birch started to drop into [his] room to talk about the causes of inflation, [he] started to drop into his, and when [they] conferred with the Chancellor, [they] found [they]'d all come to the same conclusion" (Cooper 2011, 240).

MUTUAL INFLUENCE: A SHARING OF MONETARIST PRINCIPLES

> The hand of Powell, and of the strict moral code that would come to be known as Powellism, are blatantly apparent in those words, despite Powell's own repeated protestations that he had not egged Thorneycroft on or written his script for him. Such unbending determination not to compromise (...) was Powell's trademark, and until now he had practised it almost uniquely among his colleagues in the Macmillan Government. (Heffer 1999, 227)

Different testimonies from Treasury civil servants support Heffer's view, even though they all highlight Powell's negative influence on the Chancellor. For instance, Sir Roger Makins wrote about the two Treasury secretaries' pressure on Thorneycroft just before their resignations: "Tempers were rising over the Chancellor's determination to get the estimates down at any cost. He was being egged on by Birch and Powell, who in their different ways are both rather mad" (Cairncross 1991, 143). Sir Robert Hall contended that "Powell [was] a very queer man, fanatically holding principles of economy and austerity which he [did] not understand in the least" (Cairncross 1991, 144). Yet, Chris Cooper has recently argued that Thorneycroft was not at all "a passive player" (Cooper 2011, 239), rejecting Heffer's analysis that depicted a Chancellor "under Powell's constant tutelage" (Heffer, 1999, 227). According to Cooper, Thorneycroft had real monetarist inclinations since he had constantly put forward the idea that only the control of the money supply was an effective remedy to inflation:

> It is not the making of wage claims but the printing of money to grant them which feeds the wage-price spiral. (...) True greatness does not lie in constantly attempting a range of projects (...) beyond the resources at our command. Our greatness depends on demonstrating that we are masters in our own house, that we are in control of our own currency, that we can meet our liabilities, honour our debts, and sustain the value of our money. (Cooper 2011, 237)

Thorneycroft made the decision to resign on his own and told his two secretaries that "that [did not] mean [they] [had] to go too" (Shepherd 1997, 178; Cooper 2011, 240). Powell corroborated this and recalled how the triumvirate came to the consensual decision to all resign in a theatrical way:

> [Peter Thorneycroft] said that's what we are offered, we've got to decide whether it's good enough and I remember I said shall we vote as the junior barons do in the House of Lords or used to. So [Peter Thorneycroft] said yes let's do that and I put my hand as the Lords used to do over my heart. I said not sufficient upon my conscience, and N. Birch said I don't think it will do either and Thorneycroft said I don't think it will do either. (January 1, 1989, POLL 5/35)

The Spectator added that Birch and Powell "did not resign out of loyalty to their chief, their conviction was every bit as strong as [Mr. Thorneycroft's] that resignation was the only proper course" (January 10, 1958, POLL 3/1/14). Powell considered that their resignations marked the Prime minister and the Cabinet's failure to pursue the September 1957 emergency monetarist and deflationary measures in the long run (Shepherd 1997, 180). An examination of the Powell Papers allows for a new critical hindsight into the last Cabinet meetings in December 1957 and January 1958 before the resignations. It also unveils a fresh narrative which fills the gap in the historiography. Powell clearly identified domestic and external objectives, which are reminiscent of monetarist ones:

> I am certainly personally pledged:
> Seeking control of inflation
> Stability of £
> Limiting supply of money.
> (Powell December 1957, 2; POLL 3/2/1/2)

Powell thought it right to cut down welfare expenditure, as he was convinced that there would inexorably be higher wage claims, except if inflation was held down. He advocated to keep public spending in check and especially condemned the Minister of Defence's increasing budget. If Britain was to have a leading and prestigious role and influence in the world, she had to preserve the sterling to keep international confidence and give up on too costly an Empire (Powell December 1957, 3–5; POLL 3/2/1/2):

> The Tory party must be cured of the British Empire, of the pitiful yearning to cling to the relics of a bygone system. (...) Economically and politically, we need what the Younger Pitt of 1784 stands for: what (and why) the Empire was and what (if anything) the Commonwealth is, must be made clear to ourselves till it hurts no longer. (PSG (57) 2, February 13, 1957; POLL 3/2/1/2)

Moreover, Powell reasserted his determination—which was congruent to that of his Chancellor—to uphold the golden rule and not to undermine the beneficial impact of the September 1957 monetarist measures:

> MY OWN POSITION AND THAT OF TREASURY
> Not prepared approve estimates 1958/1959
> Above the level spent in 57/58
> In other words put Government current expenditure i.e.
> Public expenditure and bank advances.
> (Powell December 1957, 5; POLL 3/2/1/2)

He also listed all the tools that the Treasury could use to achieve the goals:

1. Requires pruning of existing estimates
To eliminate virtually all new and
Additional uncommitted expenditure
2. Policy decisions on civil estimates
Which will with help of above secure
Savings of the order of £100m to £120m.
3. Such proposed additional Defense savings
As may be needed to complete Balances.
(Powell December 1957, 5; POLL 3/2/1/2)

Thorneycroft supported Powell's financial assessment of the budget estimates as he had been the root of the September 1957 measures and urged the Cabinet to comply with the golden rule (The Chancellor January 4, 1958, 1; POLL 3/2/1/2):

My colleagues will no doubt understand my attitude, however much they may deplore the need for difficult decisions which flow from it, when I say that I cannot in any circumstances approve estimates of this magnitude. (NA, PRO CAB 129/90, C.(57)295, December 27, 1957, 1)

Thorneycroft was aware of the difficulty of matching domestic goals (to maintain cost-effective and quality social services) with external ones (prestige, deployment of British troops throughout the world and nuclear deterrent]. He gave Powell the responsibility of taking stock of budget estimates and of finding significant and relevant cuts. Powell did his utmost to achieve the target, as is shown by a wide range of statistical data among his papers (POLL 3/1/16). It is worth noticing that on the eve of resignations, Powell put the external objective on top of the agenda, despite the unpopular measures that the Conservative Party would have to take:

WHAT TRYING TO DO
Hold value of pound sterling here and outside
If fail, if go on sliding
No future for either Party or country
WE AGREED TO HOLD IT
To put the pound first
Unpopular even brutal decisions.
(Powell January 5, 1958, 1; POLL 3/2/1/2)

In the light of the Chancellor's memoranda and the Cabinet meeting minutes held in the National Archives, London, and of the Powell Papers, it is possible to argue that both Powell and Thorneycroft played an active role in promoting monetarist ideas designed to control the money supply. They exerted mutual influence on each other as they tried to win the same battle of ideas. Indeed, Powell claimed: "We have each come to the same conclusions independently and spontaneously. We had looked from very separate angles at the economic problems of the country and the issues involved" (POLL 3/1/14).

POWELL'S (UN)OFFICIAL REASONS FOR RESIGNATION: DISCLOSING A DISCREPANCY

Powell considered his resignation from the Treasury as "a great turning point or crisis in his life" (POLL 3/1/14). He wrote an article, which was released the next day in the press to account for the official reason which led him to quit:

> The most certain inflationary force was that the total of the Government's commitments exceeded the total of what was brought in by taxation and borrowing. (...) The issue was not family allowances or any other specific item of welfare expenditure. The issue was whether Mr. Thorneycroft felt he had the necessary minimum support from his colleagues for the policy to which he and they were committed. He was forced to the conclusion that he had not that support. (POLL 3/1/14)

He reasserted his position in a speech he addressed to his constituents on January 9, 1959 and added:

> Government 'print money' causes inflation. The crux of our position is that, until confidence in £ and economic future restored, the amount the Government can borrow is very strictly limited. It would be criminal to gamble on being able to borrow more next year than this. (Powell January 9, 1958, 1–2; POLL 3/1/16)

However, he decided to write a secret document on January 22, 1958 in order to give up the actual reasons leading him to resign from the Treasury (January 22, 1958; POLL 3/1/16). This document is held in the Powell

Papers, Cambridge, and no biographers, but Simon Heffer to a lesser extent, have mentioned it. This new source is of paramount importance for Powell was deeply convinced that his resignation marked a watershed in the intellectual history of the Conservative Party, which, retrospectively, paved the way for Thatcher's vindication of monetarism.

Powell confessed that a set of intertwined reasons had led him to quit, while he had publicly said to journalists that there had been a single cause: the Treasure dispute revealed an ideological divide within the Cabinet: "Parallel causes, all of which were operative: (...) the personal, the historical, the theoretical and so forth" (January 22, 1958; POLL 3/1/16). Powell lamented that the Treasury civil servants had never backed the triumvirate up when they implemented the September 1957 emergency monetarist and deflationary measures: "The implications of that policy were never analysed or understood as they should have been inside, or consequently outside the Treasury. It never got to be realised how violent a revolution in thought and policy the statement of 19 September heralded" (January 22, 1958; POLL 3/1/16). Powell also rued the Cabinet decision that aborted this radical intellectual departure: "We should have carried the dialectic further in all these directions, had we remained in office" (January 22, 1958; POLL 3/1/16). Before the September 1957 measures, inflation was said to be generated by either an increase in wages or a level of demand exceeding supply, while Powell and Thorneycroft had started to sketch a fresh analysis based on the control of the money supply. He lambasted the strategy pursued by Macmillan who created the mythical image of Supermac delivering prosperity and mass-consumerism, and the stance of the Cabinet ministers who had decided to meet trade unions' claims for higher wages:

> To the Socialist notion of voluntary or imposed restraint, which former Conservative Chancellors had not seriously criticized—the Macmillan 'plateau' was the same as the Cripps 'freeze'—was now opposed the idea of a monetary environment in which wage claims could not be granted. (January 22, 1958; POLL 3/1/16)

While the Treasury triumvirate called for an economic policy based on the control of the money supply, bank credit, and public investment (Powell January 5, 1958; POLL 3/2/1/2), Powell reckoned that some ministers did not grasp "the rudiments of public finance," which boiled down to Greek to them, as they lacked appropriate economic and financial knowledge (January 22, 1958; POLL 3/1/16).

Sir Robert Hall was neither convinced by the positive impact of the September 1957 measures, nor by the monetarist rhetoric that Thorneycroft was using: "I had been very troubled by the way [the Chancellor] said such silly things about the money supply, and I was getting uncomfortable about his rigidity on things like social services" (Cairncross 1991, 143–144). He did not share Thorneycroft's point of view as the latter's strategic decisions hinged upon "a sort of laissez-faire morality" (Cairncross 1991, 144). This "laissez-faire morality" was soon to become part and parcel of the economic tenets of Powellism as T. E. Utley put it in 1968: "The main size and function of government expenditure is the crucial factor in inflation and in economic progress" (Utley 1968, 74).

POWELL'S SECRET CORRESPONDENCE WITH DENNIS ROBERTSON

Although Dennis Robertson, an anti-Keynesian economist in Cambridge, was deeply influential on Powell's economic thought, the latter's biographers rarely mention his name while Powell publicly acknowledged that "[he] [had] enjoyed and profited from the advice and instruction of Sir Dennis Robertson" (Powell 1960, 8; Cairncross 1991, 136). Robertson contended that the issue of inflation in 1957 was worsened by the detrimental role of trade unions if the government set out to preserve the sterling:

> My specific conclusion on Wages Policy—by no means an original one—was that the preservation of the value of the currency is a task, not for the trade unions nor, for the matter of that, for the employers' associations either, but for the Monetary Authorities, and that it is a task which cannot be discharged by exhortation. (Robertson and Presley 1992, 74)

He argued that it would be impossible "to prevent wage demands from continually outstripping the growth in productivity" without a high unemployment rate, amounting to 10%. In fact, not a single government would accept this situation, because, since 1945, it had been the responsibility of government to ensure full employment and a strong sterling. He thus came to the pessimistic conclusion that "the battle against inflation must be abandoned as a lost cause" (Robertson and Presley 1992, 77). Robertson's economic thought challenged the Keynesian orthodoxy and was deemed "reactionary and almost 'fascist'" by his detractors (Robertson and Presley

1992, 10). As a matter of fact, Powell found his work inspiring and decided to start a secret correspondence with him in order to better grasp the conundrum of inflation and to find out the best economic remedies to curb it.

There is a valuable range of private letters between the two men in the Powell Papers, Cambridge, which have been untapped by historians so far. And yet this correspondence enabled Powell to better understand the crucial idea to "[damp] down demand for the Thorneycroft policy" (Powell November 17, 1958; POLL 3/1/15). Powell expressed his concerns about Macmillan's hazardous economic policy:

> I am both puzzled and alarmed by the attitude of my mate colleagues which finds expression in repeated assertions of the Prime Minister and Chancellor of the Exchequer to the effect that we shall take off the brakes as soon as possible, or as soon as stability is achieved, we shall resume expansion. If these statements mean anything, they imply a belief that stable money and economic expansion are incompatible and that measures designed to prevent the effective supply of money from increasing faster than production are inimical to economic progress. (Powell June 4, 1958; POLL 3/1/15)

Dennis Robertson was well aware that his economic stance was deemed erratic by other Keynesian economists and thus he craftily replied to Powell: "I am much better at putting doubts and difficulties than at resolving them" (Robertson June 2, 1958; POLL 3/1/15). However, he explained to Powell the relation between the money supply and economic activity:

> The amount of money may be increased without reducing its value in terms of goods and services, i.e. without causing inflation,
> a) insofar as the increase is offset by a fall in velocity
> b) to the extent that total production is rising; or
> c) to the extent of any unused resources, provided that
> i) increased production results in time to 'catch up' the new money before it increases prices; and
> ii) the tendency of prices at the time is not anyhow to increase. (Robertson June 1958; POLL 3/1/15)

Powell supported the view that, since 1956, the government's goal had been to reduce demand, but he justified the economic policy he had implemented with Thorneycroft in the following way: "It seems to me unfair to designate a policy by one of its incidental and not wholly inevitable by-products, rather than by its deliberate and avowed intention" (Powell September 15, 1958; POLL 3/1/15). In other words, Powell disputed the link between economic growth and government's policy on the one hand, and that between the slackening of economic growth and government's policy on the other hand. To put it in a nutshell, Powell dismissed Macmillan's economic doctrine, which had basically consisted in pursuing a policy of stop and go since 1956:

> Granted that a Government can increase demand and thus pro-
> duction by increasing the effective money supply, surely the prin-
> cipal (and only healthy) causes of increase in production are real
> and natural, e.g. advances in techniques of production and distri-
> bution, the simultaneous increase of the power to produce and
> the desire to consume etc. Current public discussions (...) seem
> to imply that "expansion" depends on Government action, and
> that if Governments don't bring it about, nothing else will. (...)
> I would think it worth stressing that, just as "contraction" can
> come about without the help of Governments, so equally (and
> indeed, a fortiori, it being the natural trend) does "expansion."
> (Powell September 15, 1958; POLL 3/1/15)

In Robertson's view, if the Gross National Product (GNP) did not steadily rise, the best option would be to cut its growth rate without getting a zero economic growth, but he did not conceal from Powell that this assumption should be underpinned by an intricate establishment of a template: "All this is difficult to put precisely in ordinary language and without using mathe-matical expressions such as first and second differentials" (Robertson November 11, 1958; POLL 3/1/15). For Powell, the crux of the problem was to grasp the meaning of "demand reduction":

> The phrase we have used most often (...) is "damping down de-
> mand", which I think may be interpreted as "reducing the rate of
> increase of G. N. P. by means some of which may even involve
> reducing the absolute level of some components thereof." I do
> not think it is really open even to H. M. G. as at present consti-
> tuted, still less to the late lamented Thorneycroft wing thereof, to
> deny that they were trying to "damp down demand." (Robertson
> November 11, 1958; POLL 3/1/15)

As for the link between public expenditure, prices, and output, Robertson reasserted that trade unions played a harmful role in the economic decision-making process and added: "damping down of demand will eventuate in some damping down of output; and any Government or Monetary Authority which undertakes a "damping down of demand" must be held to realise that this will be the case" (Robertson November 11, 1958; POLL 3/1/15).

As Powell was eager to push further his reflections on inflation and on damping down of demand, he planned to meet Robertson in Cambridge (Powell November 17, 1958; POLL 3/1/15). The absence of further material in the Powell Papers makes it impossible to disclose the end of this secret correspondence. However, given the content of the private letters between Powell and Robertson quoted above, one has to come to the conclusion that Thorneycroft's economic policy turned out to Keynesian demand management rather than a monetarist policy.

THATCHER'S SECRET INTELLECTUAL DEBT TO POWELL

When the Treasury triumvirate resigned, Thatcher did not feel comfortable with that and stayed away. She did not approve of Macmillan's strategy designed to promote prosperity and mass-consumerism but saw that it had borne fruit, with Supermac staying in power until 1963 (Thatcher 1995, 92). Since the 1960s, Thatcher had attempted to make the problem of inflation out and she clearly became converted to monetarist ideas when she said in 1968: "We now put so much emphasis on the control of incomes that we have too little regard for the essential role of government which is the control of the money supply and management of demand" (Campbell 2001, 185). Some biographers noticed that Thatcher's September 1968 speech followed the logic of Powell's 1967 speech in Halifax (Wapshott 1983, 89–90). According to John Campbell, this meant that Thatcher had clearly been a preacher of Powellism (Campbell 2001, 186). Indeed, Thatcher usually attended Powell's speeches in the 1960s and she even replaced him at the Economic Dining Club (a free market pressure group within the Conservative Party) in 1974; which, for some historians, outlined a direct filiation of Thatcher's economic ideas to Powellism (Vinen 2009, 46).

Robert Shepherd has noted the importance that Margaret Thatcher, when she became Prime Minister in May 1979, ascribed to the 1958 Treasury resignations to advocate a radical break with the Macmillan years and the thesis of the post-war consensus:

> Powell's view that 1957–1958 marked a turning point for the British economy has been mythologized by Margaret Thatcher and her monetarist heirs on the new right. They have demonized Macmillan's Government as an inflationist and, in effect, a socialist regime, while portraying Powell, Birch and Thorneycroft as heroic martyrs. (Shepherd 1997, 164)

He thought that Thatcher managed to make Powell's ideas on inflation more popular in the 1980s, even though she never paid tribute to him during his lifetime. There were two reasons for this. Firstly, he was not a member of the Conservative Party any longer, so Thatcher had no intention to appoint him to her Cabinet in case of victory. Secondly, Powell was considered "literally mad" by a large majority of politicians (Vinen 2009, 50). However, after his death, Thatcher eventually acknowledged her intellectual debt to him: "I would say, economically we both hold the same views and I originally got them from Enoch. He was the first to realise that inflation is to do with the money supply. Enoch was marvellous at putting policy across" (Thatcher November 11, 1995; POLL 3/2/5/11).

In 1988, Powell answered a journalist who wanted to know whether or not he could see a parallel between his Treasury resignation in 1958 and Thatcher's economic policy:

> I think we are increasingly seeing that because in the last 10 years, we have seen the working out of the principle of defeating inflation by controlling the money supply which was first attempted by Thorneycroft and his colleagues in 1957. The acceptance of that diagnosis of inflation has transformed the potentiality of politics. (Powell 1989; POLL 5/35)

He put forward the idea that there was well and truly a legacy of Powellism in Thatcher's monetarist ideas: "We were Thatcherites before Thatcher's time at any rate and the term 'monetarism' had not got coming to vogue nor yet consequently been debased" (Powell 1989; POLL 5/35). According to him, she had professed "the Powellite identification of the cause of inflation" and managed to apply Milton Friedman's monetarist ideas to the very case of Britain. In this regard, Powell proudly claimed: "Milton Friedman should have shared his Nobel Prize for economics as he had purloined his monetarist theories from me" (Powell November 11, 1995; POLL 3/2/5/11). He considered that Thatcher had enhanced his own monetarist analysis on inflation by taking into account two important factors after 1979—that is the pound exchange rate and the power of trade unions:

> Monetarism was doubly the key to this. It destroyed the myth that co-operation from the trade unions was indispensable to any government for controlling inflation; and by pointing to public expenditure and government borrowing as the true causes of monetary expansion it placed the trade unions in a situation of impotence which could no longer be concealed from their own members. (Kavanagh and Seldon 1989, 83)

As a result, Thatcher could use a deep-seated economic doctrine that ruled out any form of income policy or inflation-generating wage claims preventing trade unions from interfering in the economic decision-making process to the detriment of market forces. She had become a fully equipped monetarist, keeping secret her debt to Powell for a long time.

CONCLUSIVE REMARKS: THE IMMEDIATE AFTERMATH OF THE TREASURY RESIGNATIONS REVISITED OR HOW POWELL SECRETLY PREPARED HIS RETURN TO THE CABINET IN 1960

When the Treasury triumvirate resigned on January 6, 1958, the government got panic-stricken (January 6, 1958; POLL 3/1/16). In the very short term, the Cabinet's strategy consisted in reassuring the sterling area countries to avoid an economic and financial crisis in the United Kingdom. Mr. Percy informed Macmillan: "It is most important that both Governments and public in Commonwealth countries should be immediately reassured that Mr. Thorneycroft's resignation does not represent any weakening at all in the anti-inflationary policies adopted by UK Government last September or of their determination to uphold the strength of sterling" (NA, PRO PREM 11/2421). As a result, many telegrams were immediately sent to Commonwealth leaders, with a copy of Macmillan's official response to the Treasury resignations, to reaffirm his government's determination to cope with public expenditure and to preserve the sterling. The Prime Minister nonchalantly qualified their decisions as "local difficulties." As for the new Chancellor, Derick Heathcoat Amory, he clearly accounted for his economic policy: "The change of Chancellor means no change in the Government's economic or financial policy" [*The Times* January 7, 1958; POLL 3/1/14]. Macmillan's strategy paid off as the Conservative parliamentary group and the Conservative Party, as well as the City, publicly expressed their support to the government.

Just after the Treasury triumvirate explained the reasons for their resignation in the press, a senior figure of the Conservative Party noticed that they had not sought to carry out a revolution within the party and bring down the Prime Minister:

> For the present I feel we can write off the danger of a revolt. Nigel flapped as usual nosily and somewhat irresponsibly in his constituency last night, but I fancy this will be the last instalment for the time being at least before Parliament meets. (Simpson January 16, 1958; NA, PRO PREM 11/2421)

Although Edward Heath expressed doubts about this in the 1980s (January 1, 1989; POLL 5/35), for the time being, as shown above, Powell let the press know in January 1957 that he had no intention to jeopardize Cabinet policies:

> On one thing I am absolutely determined. I will say and do nothing which will in anyway weaken or embarrass the Government. (...) It will be my endeavour by word and deed, and perhaps more by silence to give my utmost support to the Government despite all that has passed. (POLL 3/1/14)

After his resignation from the Treasury, Powell continued to analyze the problem of inflation and the effective remedies to handle it. That is the reason why he started a secret correspondence with anti-Keynesian economist Dennis Robertson about the dangers of inflation—"[One of the] escalators which takes traditional Treasury control 'for a ride'" (Powell April 1958, 217). However, his private correspondence revealed that the monetary policy he implemented with Thorneycroft boiled down to managing demand in a Keynesian perspective instead of pursuing a monetarist policy.

The situation changed in 1959 when Macmillan led his campaign on the theme of prosperity and unprecedented mass-consumerism. It resulted in the Prime Minister's dismissal of Powell's budget rectitude. Consequently,

Powell was anticipating a substantial increase in public expenditure and budget estimates and resolved to debunk Supermac's prosperity myth:

> If this belief can be proved and plausibly argued, to be baseless, then greater sympathy would be perfect with those who have opposed increased expenditure, and less with a policy which bids fair to advice Budget estimates showing a record increase in each of these excessive years. (Powell January 22, 1959; POLL 3/1/14)

In addition, Powell explained to Thorneycroft that since their resignations, Britain's economic situation had neither supported their economic analysis nor their 1957 golden rule:

> The majority inside and outside the house take it as axiomatic that we were wrong, because anything has gone well since then—retail price index, reserves, balance of payments—and the danger has appeared to be recession rather than boom. Even to the small minority who do not share this oversimplification, the issues which divided us from our colleagues seem of little more than historical interest. (Powell February 21, 1959; POLL 3/1/14)

That was the very moment when Powell exerted his influence on Thorneycroft to urge him to help him criticize government policies and overhaul their golden rule:

> In these circumstances, I believe that it would now be a mistake to refrain from comment and criticism of financial and economic policy as occasion arises or can be made. Above all, I submit that it would be mistaken for you now to appear to make foreign affairs your concern. (...) The interpretation would be put on this that you admit you were wrong as Chancellor and are trying for a fresh start in a different field. (Powell February 21, 1959; POLL 3/1/14)

Robert Shepherd points out that Powell led an effective campaign for the October 1959 General election, and since he made an indictment of the April 1958 budget, he had converted many politicians to the idea of controlling the public spending increase. Powell had become a rebel within his party and by making public the weakness of Macmillan's policy, he had managed to become an influential political figure, who was seen as clear-headed, experienced and skillful by the right wing of his party (Shepherd 1997, 201). Macmillan was aware of the danger looming ahead and decided to appoint Powell and Thorneycroft to great spending Departments (Cooper 2011, 242), whose budget estimates would be hard to reduce. Therefore, Powell became Minister of Health on July 27, 1960. In his view, it was better to compel Powell to comply with collective discipline and responsibility if he was part of his Cabinet. He thus deterred him from revealing to the public the secrecy of an ideological divide that was to widen in the 1970s. Once again, after his 1959 landslide victory and solving the Powell-Thorneycroft issue, he could triumphantly "tell the newcomers [among his parliamentary group] not to be afraid of being rebels" (Clarke et al. 2015, 270). That was Macmillan's last act of political art in the 1950s.

BIBLIOGRAPHY

Primary sources

Archives

The Powell Papers, Churchill College, Cambridge

  POLL 3/1/14

  POLL 3/1/15

  POLL 3/1/16

  POLL 3/2/1/2

  POLL 3/2/4/13

  POLL 3/2/5/11

  POLL 3/2/1/2

  POLL 5/35

Cabinet Papers, The National Archives, Kew, London

  NA, PRO CAB 128/32

  NA, PRO CAB 130/139

The Prime Minister Papers, The National Archives, Kew, London

NA, PRO PREM 11/2306

NA, PRO PREM 11/2421

NA, PRO, PREM 11/2973

The Treasury Papers, The National Archives, Kew, London

NA, PRO T 227/1116

NA, PRO T 227/485

British Oral Archive of Political and Administrative History, LSE Archives, London

Published sources

Powell, Enoch. 1958. "Treasury Control in the Age of Inflation." *The Banker* CVIII (387): 216–219.

Powell, Enoch. 1960. *Saving in a Free Society*. London: Hutchinson.

Powell, Enoch. 1980. "Superwhig?" *The Spectator*, March 1 : 18.

Secondary sources

[A. N]. 1958. "At the End of the Queue." *The Spectator*, January 17: 64.

Bale, Tim. 2012. *The Conservatives since 1945 (The Drivers of Party Change)*. Oxford: OUP.

Cairncross, Alec (ed.). 1991. *The Robert Hall Diaries 1954–1961*. London: Unwin Hyman.

Campbell, John. 2001. *Margaret Thatcher, Volume I: The Grocer's Daughter*. London: Pimlico.

Carr, Richard, and Bradley W. Hart. 2013. *The Foundations of the British Conservative Party*. London: Bloomsbury.

Clarke, Peter. 1992. *A Question of Leadership, From Gladstone to Thatcher*. London: Penguin.

Clarke, Charles, Toby S. James, Tim Bale, and Patrick Diamond. 2015. *British Conservative Leaders?* London: Biteback Publishing.

Cockett, Richard. 1995. *Thinking the Unthinkable: Think-Tanks and the Economic Counter-Revolution, 1931–1983.* London: Fontana Press.

Cooper, Chris. 2011. "Little Local Difficulties Revisited: Peter Thorneycroft, the 1958 Treasury Resignations and the Origins of Thatcherism." *Contemporary British History* 25 (2): 227–250.

Dell, Edmund. 1997. *The Chancellors, A History of the Chancellors of the Exchequer, 1945–1990.* London: HarperCollins.

Gabis, Stanley T. 1978. "Political Secrecy and Cultural Conflict. A Plea for Formalism." *Administration and Society* 10 (2): 139–175.

Garnett, Mark, and Kevin Hickson. 2009. *Conservative Thinkers (The Key Contributors to the Political Thought of the Modern Conservative Party).* Manchester: MUP.

Green, E. H. H. 2002. *Ideologies of Conservatism.* Oxford: Oxford University Press.

Harris, Robin. 2011. *The Conservatives (A History).* London: Transworld Publishers.

Heffer, Simon. 1999. *Like the Roman, The Life of Enoch Powell.* London: Phoenix Giant.

Hennessy, Peter. 2006. *Having so Good, Britain in the Fifties.* London: Allen Lane.

Horn, Eva. 2006. "Actors/Agents: Bertolt Brecht and the Politics of Secrecy." *Grey Room* 24: 38–55.

Horne, Alistair. 1989. *Macmillan 1957–1986, Vol II of the Official Biography.* London: Macmillan.

Jarvis, Matthew. 1995. "The 1958 Treasury Dispute and the Nature of Conservatism." Unpublished MA dissertation, University of Leeds, 98p.

Kavanagh, Denis, and Anthony Seldon (eds.). 1989. *The Thatcher Effect.* Oxford: Oxford University Press.

Lamb, Richard. 1995. *The Macmillan Years: The Emerging Truth*. London: John Murray.

Lowe, Rodney. 1989. "Resignations at the Treasury: The Social Services Committee and the Failure to Reform the Welfare State, 1955–57." *Journal of Social Policy* 18: 505–526.

Macmillan, Harold. 1966. *The Middle Way (20 Years after)*. London: Macmillan.

Macmillan, Harold. 1971. *Riding the Storm, 1956–1959*. London: Macmillan.

Mitchell, Stuart. 2006. *The Brief and Turbulent Life of Modernising Conservatism*. Newcastle: Cambridge Scholars.

Pugh, Martin. 1994. *State and Society: British Political and Social History, 1970–1992*. London: Edward Arnold.

Ramsden, John. 1996. *Winds of Change: Macmillan to Heath*. London: Longman.

Robbins, Keith (ed.). 1990. *The Blackwell Bibliographical Dictionary of British Political Life in the Twentieth Century*. Oxford: Blackwell.

Robertson, Dennis, and John Presley. 1992. *Robertson on Economic Policy*. New York: St Martin's Press.

Sampson, Anthony. 1967. *Macmillan, A Study in Ambiguity*. London: Allen Lane.

Schofield, Camilla. 2013. *Enoch Powell and the Making of Postcolonial Britain*. Cambridge: Cambridge University Press.

Seldon, Anthony, and Stuart Ball (eds.). 1994. *Conservative Century (The Conservative Party since 1900)*. Oxford: Oxford University Press.

Shepherd, Robert. 1997. *Enoch Powell, A Biography*. London: Pimlico.

Thatcher, Margaret. 1995. *The Path to Power*. London: HarperCollins.

Turner, John. 1994. *Macmillan*. London: Longman.

Utley, T. E. 1968. *Enoch Powell (The Man and his Thinking)*. London: William Kimber.

Vinen, Richard. 2009. *Thatcher's Britain (The Politics and Social Upheaval of the Thatcher Era)*. London: Simon & Schuster.

Wapshott, Nicholas. 1983. *Thatcher*. London: Futura.

CHAPTER 4

BRITAIN'S ENERGY POLICY IN WALES: "SECRET PLAN FOR NUCLEAR POWER PLANT" (SHIPTON 2005A)

Stéphanie Bory
University Jean Moulin—Lyon 3

Secrecy has characterized the method of government in Wales ever since its incorporation by England in 1536. Any decision concerning the Welsh nation was made in London, in Westminster or in 10 Downing Street's dark corridors, and not openly in Cardiff, before being imposed on the local population. It was exactly in this way that, at the end of 1955, Welsh people were informed that Liverpool had secretly decided to build a reservoir in Wales in order to provide its factories with water. The scheme proposed to drown the Cwn Celyn Valley, near Tryweryn, and to move a substantial Welsh speaking community. The local population was caught off guard by that totally unexpected decision, as illustrated by the following testimony given by Mrs Harriet Parry, the village postwoman, in Roy Clews' *To Dream of Freedom. The Struggle of MAC and the Free Wales Army*: "Then one day, Bethan, my daughter was about only 10 years old and she came from school, and when we were having our tea she said [...] 'They going to drown this village Mam, and the fields, and everything'" (Clews 1980, 11). Using "they" in this quotation conjures up the impression of a faraway decision maker. Wales thus suffered from a democratic deficit for many decades during which Welsh people voted in large numbers for the Labour Party and yet were subject to Margaret Thatcher's liberal policy via Secretaries of State for Wales who were both Conservative and very often English. Following the 1987 General Election which represented the Conservatives' third victory in a row, slogans such as "We voted Labour—we got Thatcher" could be seen scrawled on walls. The *Western Mail*, a Welsh daily newspaper, even wrote that the M4, the motorway between England and Cardiff, was the only link between Cardiff and John Redwood, Secretary of State for Wales from 1993 to 1995 in the Major government.

It is in the field of nuclear energy, a long-lasting bone of contention between Cardiff and London, that the theme of secrecy has been most present, ever since the 1950s, a decade which witnessed the building of the first nuclear power station in Wales. This scheme in Trawsfynydd, situated in the center of Snowdonia National Park, had already caused deep anger in Wales, since once again people were excluded from talks and debates organized in the greatest secrecy in London, without consulting the population that was directly concerned. The building a few years later of the Wylfa nuclear power station on Anglesey followed the same pattern. Welsh people could not make their own decisions for their own country.

To end this way of governing based on secrecy and opaqueness, Wales decided at the end of the twentieth century to introduce a different political culture in the National Assembly for Wales set up by the *Government of Wales Act 1998*. The new institutions were to be responsible, credible, and, last but not least, transparent. Secrecy and private settlements were supposed to belong to the past and the new authorities were to work in the open.

However, the development of nuclear energy still seems to be a state secret, be it British or Welsh. Indeed, at the end of 2005, rumor had it that the Blair administration nursed a secret plan to set up a new power station in Wales as part of a more global nuclear renewal scheme. On December 30, 2005, the *Western Mail* published an article entitled "Secret Plan for Nuclear Power Plant". Martin Shipton, the journalist who wrote the article, had recourse to a high-ranking source from the Energy Department to denounce and shed light on this plan. The very following day, the British government counter-attacked with a letter signed by Malcolm Wicks, the Energy Secretary of State, and published in the same newspaper. It was thus thanks to the Welsh press that people in Wales learnt that London had decided to renew its nuclear sector, a move confirmed on May 16, 2006 by Prime Minister Tony Blair himself, addressing businessmen in London, not in Cardiff, despite the Welsh population and government's opposition to this type of energy. But it was also the presswhich, at the beginning of 2012, unveiled the u-turn of that same government which now supports the new nuclear building in Wylfa. Such a decision was made public on March 14, 2012 by Welsh First Minister Carwyn Jones and Welsh Environment Minister John Griffiths in a document entitled *Energy Wales: A Low Carbon Transition*. The Welsh government's credibility was then itself questioned. It may be wondered whether it adopted and applied the same practices as its British

ESEESE

---

counterpart and hence if it decided to lie to Welsh voters. Is nuclear energy so burning and controversial an issue that it implies having recourse to secrecy, even lying?

This article aims to study how the British government may have used secrecy in order to avoid conflicts with the periphery, to the detriment of democracy, a policy regularly denounced by the local press, and to consider the reasons why the Welsh government, which had committed to transparency, seems to have adopted the same practices. The two systems of government, the British one apparently based on secrecy and the Welsh one on transparency and openness will first be presented. Britain's current energy policy in Wales will then be analyzed, with a focus first on London's strategy, then on Cardiff's.

1. SECRECY VERSUS TRANSPARENCY: TWO SYSTEMS OF GOVERNANCE

The British Government and Secrecy: A Tradition

Wales and Scotland have always suffered from a democratic deficit ever since they have been united with England. Hence, both countries have been submitted to a political system in which secrecy traditionally prevailed. This could partly be due to the undeniable distance between the political center, London, and the periphery, Cardiff, and thus by communication problems. Leopold Kohr, an Austrian philosopher and political theorist who taught at Aberystwyth University from 1968 onwards, defined the "theory of size" in *The Breakdown of Nations*, first published in 1957. He applied this principle to Britain, which was, in his opinion, oversized. As a result, the periphery was isolated and disconnected from the center: "Effective power, like sound or light, diminishes as distance increases" (Kohr 2012, 46). Kohr, therefore, advised ill-informed Wales to secede from Britain, explaining in the preface to the 1986 edition that "politically, centralized states such as Spain or Great Britain will have to come to terms with small-state nationalism and regional devolution under the pressure of inspired leaders such as Gwynfor Evans[1] of Wales" (10), but being at the same time convinced that, in the 1980s, London's strategy consisted in keeping control over Wales, to manage and spare it, but to the detriment of democracy, as he indicated,

---

1   Gwynfor Evans (1912–2005) was the president of Plaid Cymru, the Welsh nationalist party, from 1945 to 1981. He was elected MP for Carmarthen in 1966.

later in his work: "There are similar attempts at *national* reorganization in Scotland and Wales. Should they succeed also, it would mean the end of the United Kingdom altogether. It would break the small county organization which now enables London to rule effectively in all corners of the British Isles" (189). Such a democratic deficit was deeply felt in the 1980s, when Prime Minister Margaret Thatcher set up many quasi non-governmental organizations called Quangos. She aimed to control Wales by granting the nation administrative devolution. She was definitely not ready to really devolve matters dealt with by central power:

> The Rt. Hon. Mrs. Margaret Thatcher, Prime Minister of Britain, may be "all in favour of smallness in government". But tell her that the only way to reduce the size of government is by reducing the size of the unit to be governed, as is demanded by the regional devolutionists, and she will consider the very thought as an attack on the sacred unity of Great Britain, which is about the last thing the United Kingdom can afford any longer. (11)

That was why Kohr was aware powerful states would never agree to be dismantled.

Such a policy of secrecy was especially implemented when it was decided to build two nuclear power stations in Wales in the 1950s and 1960s. The schemes were adopted without the consent of the local population. A first decision was made quite secretly in London in 1957 within a context of energy dependence and energy supply instability, following the Suez Crisis in 1956: a nuclear power station was to be built in Trawsfynydd, Wales. During a debate in the House of Lords on January 30, 1957, Lord Lawson regretted such lack of transparency: "These matters were decided by people who were little known to the country, and without any consultation with Parliament— work which was practically directing the course of a new industrial revolution" (*The Times* January 1957). Similarly, Welsh MPs asked to be consulted on the issue. After a feasibility study, which went on for several months, the government delayed its decision due to discussions between green associations, seeking to defend the landscape, and the British government. Indeed, the selected site was situated in the center of Snowdonia National Park, created in 1951 following the 1949 National Parks and Access to the Countryside Act. So, people had the feeling that decisions were made far away by strangers, without any communication or dialogue, as indicated by the following quotation, also by Lord Lawson, but during another debate in March 1957:

It had been decided to site certain stations in the more remote areas, some of them conflicting with the National Parks Act, and not in built up areas. [...] The government should say whether in principle the national parks and areas of outstanding beauty would be avoided and that the electricity authority would consult the National Parks Commission in the earliest stages of their exploration of sites in view of the duty laid on the commission to protect the countryside generally. (*The Times* March 1957, 40) (my emphasis)

Lord Lawson's use of the passive form at the beginning of the quote emphasizes the helplessness of the local population, all the more so as he clearly calls for communication and consultation in the second part. He raises here another issue: the siting of a nuclear station in a rural area, and not close to industrial areas. He was joined by Lord Chorley, the honorary secretary of the Council for the Protection of Rural England (CPRE), who declared on that same day in the House of Lords: "There was no reason why the nuclear power stations should not be built in the areas where industrial expansion had taken place, and where the electricity was needed". It may be wondered where the areas he was mentioning were situated. Certainly not in Wales, a predominantly rural country where the only industrial sectors of activity were then coal mining and slate quarrying. In England probably, but following the incident at Windscale, later called Sellafield, on October 10, 1957[2], English people rejected the building of a station. As a result, the rationale of the development of nuclear stations in Wales, as well as the arguments used to justify their siting, was covered in secrecy and raised many questions.

Welsh people, however, desperately needed jobs, and they felt excluded from the discussions, as indicated by the following article from *The Times*:

[But] it is not the only consideration. The right of the local inhabitants to maintain themselves prosperously within a park has never been questioned. And in Snowdonia that right takes a special form. The area is one in which the chief industry, slate quarrying, has declined heavily and may decline further, so that many of the people are faced with the choice of finding new work locally or leaving their homes. (*The Times* 1958, 9)

2 The Windscale fire of October 10, 1957 was the worst nuclear accident in Great Britain's history, ranked in severity at level 5 on the 7-point International Nuclear Event Scale.

Social considerations thus had to be taken into account. The station was finally built and started working in February 1965, just as a second scheme came into being.

That episode is an illustration of the reasons why Welsh people asked for self-government for many decades. In 1997, following a referendum organized by the Blair government, they obtained the creation of the National Assembly for Wales (NAW), with Assembly Members (AMs) elected for the first time 2 years later and able to implement a different system of governance, one based on openness and transparency.

Wales' Longing for Openness and Transparency

When Ron Davies, then Secretary of State for Wales in the Blair government, considered the future Welsh assembly in September 1997, he had a very precise idea of the future body: "A new institution that will both herald a new style of more inclusive politics that better fits the needs and character of Wales and open to public scrutiny and accountability the machinery of government in Wales" (Davies, in Wigley 2001). His vision of a new form of political culture included all the major characteristics of the NAW, set up thanks to the *Government of Wales Act 1998*: it was to be responsible, credible, and transparent. It is the only body that can implement policies and programmes devised by Welsh people for Welsh people. In *The Legacy Report 2007–2011* published in 2011, the NAW is described in the following way: "The National Assembly for Wales is the democratically elected body that represents the interests of Wales and its people, makes laws for Wales and holds the Welsh government to account" (NAW 2011, 4). As clearly stated in the quotation, the NAW wants to be totally transparent. To achieve this objective, it must allow Welsh citizens to have access to its work and take part in its governing process, a duty emphasized as early as 2000, when a users' guide was published by Lord Dafydd Elis-Thomas, then its Presiding Officer:

> The need to create a culture of openness where participation is the key, places a specific duty upon the Office of the Presiding Officer to ensure that the Assembly is accessible to all the people of Wales. [...] This book is a significant contribution to the open door policy we have pursued and should serve to encourage all the people of Wales to contribute to our new process of government. (NAW 2000, 7)

Secrecy and private settlements were supposed to belong to the past and the new authorities were to work in the open, as illustrated by the very architecture of the *Senedd*.

The new building, inaugurated in 2006, encapsulated such longing for openness and transparency promoted by the founding fathers of the NAW. It works as a metonymic place since Richard Rogers, the architect selected for the scheme, designed it as an open space, inviting people to participate in the democratic process. A square and some steps make the link between the place and the population. Ivan Harbour, the architect working in partnership with the Rogers agency, explained in an article published in the French magazine *Le Monde 2* on November 24, 2007 and entitled "À Cardiff, la démocratie en toute clarté": "This is a building which says: Please, come in!" (Harbour, in Champenois 2007, 57). This is a success since visitors, after walking through an inconspicuous checkpoint, have access to all, or nearly all, the building. Many panels are glass, to show the transparency of the place. Two levels out of three are open to the public who can attend debates in the chamber, the *Siambr*. The very description given on the website of the NAW highlights this will for transparency: "Transparent at the public level, the debates take place below within the slate plinth. The *Senedd* was designed to be as open and accessible as possible" (NAW 2012). More than 100,000 people visited the building in 4 months after it was inaugurated and it celebrated its 500,000th visitor in October 2007.

Finally, the Welsh institutions are characterized by a digital transparency, since Wales is a digital democracy, operating in the most modern—technologically speaking—buildings. The country seems to be governed by an e-government, with Carwyn Jones, for instance, acting between 2002 and 2007 as the Minister for Open Government. In April 2008, Peter Black, the Liberal Democrat AM for South Wales West, launched e-petitions, which entailed a surge in the number of petitions sent to the NAW, more than 100 during the first year. At the same time, Senedd-tv was set up, as well as e-forums. In January 2010, a *BBC Democracy Live* pod was put in the *Senedd* to allow Welsh people to participate even more easily in the workings of their political system. This digital transparency is a model for Westminster: John Bercow, who was then the Speaker of the House of Commons, came to meet the NAW's Presiding Officer in September 2009 "to learn about the work of the Assembly, specifically what the Assembly is doing to encour-age more people to take part in the democratic process through the e-petitions and Senedd.tv" (NAW 2011, 19). Furthermore, the NAW is present on the Internet. Ever since the official separation of the executive and the legislative powers in May 2007, a separation unofficially operated since 2002, two different websites can be accessed: one for the Welsh Assembly Government (WAG), led by the First Minister, and the other for the NAW itself. These are very rich sites, which are updated daily. Nevertheless, such an evolution contradicts the longing for openness displayed by the NAW's founding fathers and creates tensions, as indicated by Professor Richard Rawlings who mentioned "[...] the evident tensions between a strong centralized form of decision-making and the more open and participatory process that people were led to expect in the White Paper *A Voice for Wales*" (Rawlings 2002, 11).

As a result, the Welsh system of governance seems to suffer from the effects of excessive transparency, especially when that comes into conflict with Britain's interests, as in the field of energy. Indeed, the development of nuclear energy, more particularly, still seems to be a state secret, be it British or Welsh, as evoked by Glyn Davies, the Conservative AM between 1999 and 2007 and, after January 2006, the Conservative spokesman on the environment:

> To build a new nuclear power station in Wales without the support of the Welsh people would be the modern day equivalent of flooding Tryweryn. The UK Government must convince the majority of the Welsh people that a new nuclear power station at Wylfa would be safe, cost-effective and essential for the economy. Any secret plans in place to build new nuclear generation capacity in Wales would be an outrage. [...] There must be a role for the National Assembly in the debate. (Davies, in Shipton 2005a)

Such a system of governance, based on secrecy, is still applied in Wales in the early twenty-first century, despite the creation of the NAW and its pledges to be transparent, as a study of Britain's current energy policy in Wales will demonstrate.

2. BRITAIN'S ENERGY POLICY IN WALES

London's Strategy

It is first necessary to study London's energy strategy since energy production is only partially devolved: the NAW can make the final decision only for schemes producing less than 50 MW. In February 2003, a white paper entitled *Our Energy Future—Creating a low-carbon economy* was published in Britain. The Blair government committed firstly to save energy through energy efficiency, and secondly to promote renewables in order to cut greenhouse gas emissions by 60% by 2020. It seemed then that nuclear energy was put aside since the government could not afford to finance both research and development in renewables and the building of new nuclear power stations:

> Although nuclear power produces no carbon dioxide, its current economics make new nuclear build an unattractive option and there are important issues of nuclear waste to be resolved. Against the background, we conclude it is right to concentrate our efforts on energy efficiency and renewables. We do not, therefore, propose to support new nuclear build now. But we will keep the option open. (Great Britain 2003, 44)

Yet, the British government did not conceal the fact that it kept the possibility of changing its strategy.

At the end of 2005, rumor had it that the British administration nursed a secret plan to set up a new power station in Wales as part of a more global nuclear renewal scheme. Indeed, as the press then revealed, the Prime Minister was said to have asked Energy Minister Malcolm Wicks and DTI Minister Alan Johnson to call for a new study on energy to update the 2003 white paper. A consultation phase was due to take place between January 23 and April 14, 2006. But for journalists and environmentalists, it was clear Tony Blair had already secretly made his decision, as indicated by Julian Rosser, Friends of the Earth Cymru (FoE Cymru) chair:

> It's been very clear that Tony Blair has made his mind up for quite a few years. [...] Setting up the review in the first place was a suspicious thing to do given the first review was very clearly saying nuclear power was uneconomic and not something to pursue. (Rosser, in Withers 2006)

SECRETS & LIES IN THE UNITED KINGDOM

Tony Blair's secret plans were thus unveiled, and on December 30, 2005, even before the consultation started, the *Western Mail* published an article entitled "Secret Plan for Nuclear Power Plant". The following day, the British government counter-attacked with a letter signed by Malcolm Wicks and published in the same newspaper, in which he favored nuclear energy for the sake of sustainable development and climate change:

> Contrary to the opinion of the *Western Mail*, I have not made up my mind on nuclear and there are no "secret plans" to build a nuclear power station in Wales.

> The facts are that the Prime Minister announced an Energy Review in November to make sure we are on track to meet our goals set out in the 2003 Energy White paper, and I'm feeding that up. I'm committed to engaging the views of the public on our options for future energy supplies, nuclear is one of the options we'll look at but I'm neutral on that. As part of that review we'll also consider the role or renewables, coal and gas in any future energy mix. (Wicks, in Shipton 2005b)

It was thus the Welsh press which obliged the British government to clearly state its real and new energy policy and put an end to the secret policy implemented by London when dealing with energy.

The reasons for this change of policy must be considered. First of all, Britain had ratified the Kyoto Protocol and thus had to reach the objectives set in that document. It was clear that nuclear energy was to be part of the necessary energy mix. Furthermore, the British government delayed the announcement of the decision for populist and political reasons. Obviously, finding sites for energy facilities is always difficult insofar as nobody really feels like having a nuclear power station or a wind farm in their backyard, the famous NIMBY argument. Malcolm Wicks mentions not only nuclear but also renewable energy, yet sources were often regarded as uneven or irregular. Indeed, some sources of energy, especially wind farms, faced much opposition in England, which encouraged the government to choose Welsh places as potential sites, as indicated by the following letter sent by L. J. Jenkins, a reader of *Cambria*, and published in the special issue "The Wind Power Debate":

Wales has become, in short, a dumping ground for these hideous, noisy monstrosities because Tony Blair would not dare desecrate England's countryside in this way—England has far too many marginal seats! It is particularly ironic that the Welsh people now has to defend its country against its own idiotic politicians. (Jenkins 2006)

Statistics are revealing: Wales accounts for 8% of the United Kingdom's area and 5% of its population, but has a concentration of 34% of wind turbines, while England represents 53% of the territory, 85% of the population, but only 30% of wind turbines. There are seven times more wind turbines per km^2 and 20 times more turbines per inhabitant in Wales than in England. The government was thus trying to defend English interests. Finally, the debate on energy sources was often reduced to the following proposal: choosing between wind farms or a nuclear power station. The British government considered it was probably easier to make the Welsh accept a nuclear power station than hundreds of wind turbines, a point of view shared by Neil Crumpton, a member of FoE Cymru: "We are concerned that if the UK wind energy programme is stalled by such criticisms, then a nuclear power programme could be back on the agenda next year following the Government's current Energy Review" (Crumpton 2001). As a result, it may be questioned whether this secret plan, unveiled in the Welsh press, was a strategy devised by London in order to figure out the best energy policy, and also to avoid fierce reactions in Wales, a nuclear-free country since 1982.

On July 11, 2006, the British government published a new energy review entitled *The Energy Challenge, Energy Review Report 2006*. And yet, as early as December 2005, a campaign called Keep Wales Nuclear Free was launched by Friends of the Earth in Pembrokeshire in order to collect signatures against the building of new nuclear stations in Wales. Sundance Renewables was the first organization to rally it, quickly joined by FoE Cymru and the Centre for Alternative Technology. Alan Simpson, the Labour MP for Nottingham South, was the first MP to support the campaign, followed by Martin Caton (Gower), Paul Flynn (Newport West), and Nia Griffith (Llanelli). On January 30, 2006, Jenny Willott (Cardiff Central MP) and Mick Bates (LibDem AM for Montgomeryshire) gave a press conference in front of the NAW to ask all politicians, whatever party they belonged to, to support the petition. A document with 2,350 signatures was handed in to 10 Downing Street on April 18, 2006, even before the review was officially published. On this occasion, the Welsh press was once again instrumental in unveiling state secrets, thus allowing for reactions in Wales even before the official report was published.

In 2008, DTI Minister John Hutton confirmed the plans introduced in the 2006 energy review to build new reactors in Wales, supposedly next to old ones. Even if the National Assembly for Wales has limited powers, it can still put pressure on the British government, as stressed by Tomos Livingstone, the political editor of the *Western Mail* in January 2008:

> The decision is likely to prove highly divisive in Wales, with the Assembly Government and several Labour MPs opposed to new nuclear build. [...] A Government-commissioned report released last year under the Freedom of Information Act suggested siting new sites in England to avoid clashes with the devolved administrations, even though the Assembly Government—unlike the Scottish Executive—has no power to block a nuclear power station. (Livingstone 2008)

The final decision was made in July 2010. We may hence wonder which strategy was left to London, apart from convincing the WAG to agree with its energy plans, and to Cardiff.

Cardiff's Strategy

If London's strategy is still based on secrecy, a different policy may be expected from Wales, which has implemented a transparent system of governance. It is thus now necessary to study Cardiff's energy strategy and answer to London's.

First of all, Wales has always been traditionally opposed to nuclear energy, and the WAG, ever since the creation of the NAW, has repeatedly voiced its rejection of this type of energy production, thus respecting Welsh history. Such a stance can also be explained by the duty imposed on the Assembly to promote sustainable development, this being one of the key principles of the *GOWA 1998* and reiterated in section 79 of the *GOWA 2006*: "The Welsh Ministers must make a scheme setting out how they propose, in the exercise of their functions, to promote sustainable development". Respecting this commitment, the Welsh institutions, the Assembly and the Government, published a document entitled *Technical Advice Note 8: Planning for Renewable Energy* (2005), in which renewables were promoted and favored over and above nuclear energy. This strategy was confirmed 5 years later in *A Low Carbon Revolution—The Welsh Assembly Government Energy Policy Statement*, dealing with the advantages and drawbacks of nuclear energy and reminding readers that the WAG cannot oppose the building of nuclear stations.

The Welsh institutions' strategy had traditionally been supported by the Welsh press and the green lobby. However the latter, working as watchdogs, revealed in early 2011 that the Welsh government, especially the First Minister and Deputy First Minister, had changed their minds. On April 6, 2011, Chris Kelsey published an article entitled "From Nuclear Power to Offshore Wind, Difficult Choices for Energy Planners":

> This must be a matter of frustration for the men and women in the *Senedd*. Three years ago the Assembly Government issued a consultation on what it called its renewable energy route map, in which it asserted that within twenty years Wales could generate more electricity than it consumed, and all from renewable sources. Nuclear power did not feature in the route map, not only because the Assembly Government has no power over whether nuclear stations are built or not, but also because to the green-minded Assembly ministers nuclear energy is not a truly sustainable option in the way wind and wave power are. (Kelsey 2011)[3]

On April 25, 2011, FoE Cymru published a press release entitled "'No New Nuclear Power in Wales' Call to Ieuan and Carwyn on Chernobyl Anniversary" and stating "On the 25th anniversary of the Chernobyl disaster, party leaders Carwyn Jones and Ieuan Wyn Jones have been criticized by FoE Cymru for supporting a new nuclear power station at Wylfa. The group is also critical of the politicians for opposing their own coalition government's policy on Wylfa and, in the case of Ieuan Wyn Jones, going against the policies of the party he leads" (FoE Cymru 2011). Yet, in its manifesto *Ambition is Critical. A Manifesto for a Better Wales* published for the Welsh elections in May 2011, Plaid Cymru did not adopt a clear position on the issue and only made vague commitments such as:

---

3   Chris Kelsey quotes *Renewable Energy Route Map* published by the WAG on February 19, 2008 in which then Environment Minister Jane Davidson clearly explained: "In particular we believe that with Wales' coastline, geography and climate, it is quite feasible for us within 20 years to produce more electricity from renewables than we consume as a nation", *Renewable Energy Route Map* (WAG 2008, 1).

We will ensure that Wales becomes a pioneer of "green" technologies. We want to encourage and support the innovation and development of the products and services that a low-carbon economy demands. We will support Welsh business so it can exploit the opportunities offered by our natural resources and take a leading role in developing low-carbon and sustainable energy technologies. (Plaid Cymru 2011, 22)

In *Standing Up for Wales*, the Welsh Labour Party did not precisely commit itself either: "We will continue to seek responsibility for renewable energy consents up to 100 MW on both sea and land, enabling Wales to move quicker in providing clean energy solutions for all" (Welsh Labour Party 2011, 98). It is thus necessary to study whether nuclear energy was a taboo for Welsh politicians and if they tried to avoid a controversial subject.

In June 2011, the Welsh elections in May having returned a Labour majority in Wales, David Cameron's government announced it had decided to build new generation reactors in Wylfa, the location of the country's second station which was supposed to stop any activity more than 10 years before. After the outcry caused by the decision, there were strong reactions in Wales. But it was only in a document entitled *Energy Wales: A Low Carbon Transition*, published on March 14, 2012, that First Minister Carwyn Jones and Environment Minister John Griffiths officially supported the development of nuclear energy on Anglesey, for the very first time in the Welsh government's history:

> The development of the Horizon nuclear new build (Wylfa B) is a vital component of not just the Anglesey Energy Island Programme but of our wider energy future in providing a constant energy source to complement the intermittency of renewable sources. [...] The Welsh Government supports the development of a new nuclear power station on Anglesey. (WAG 2012, 21)

This decisive move had already been unveiled in the press 1 year before. Such a decision, announced only a few days after the first anniversary of the 2011 nuclear accident in Fukushima, Japan, was sharply criticized by defenders of the environment. This u-turn on the part of the Welsh government remains to be studied in order to question whether it had been lying to the population before.

First of all, defenders of the environment raised the issue of the limited powers held by the Welsh institutions, especially in energy since, as indicated earlier, the sector is only partially devolved. For the others, decisions are made in London. So the nuclear issue symbolizes the debate around its powers as well as its credibility, even its usefulness. This was clearly indicated by Gareth Clubb, chairing FoE Cymru in 2012, who, in a press release, was calling for more energy powers for the Welsh government:

> Wales desperately needs the power over planning and consenting for major energy infrastructure to free ourselves from the Whitehall mandarins who have no interest in Wales taking the lead in renewable jobs. Devolution of powers over energy is working for Scotland, and if we're not going to be left behind, we must see it coming to Wales. It's good for the environment, good for job creation, and it's the only way Wales can play a role in reducing our climate change emissions. That is what we need to start hearing from the Welsh Government. (Clubb 2012)

He was thereby reassessing the commitments FoE Cymru made in the document entitled *Manifesto for a Greener Wales* it published for the May 2011 elections:

> There should be no new nuclear build in Wales, as this could divert resources or political attention away from more effective low carbon solutions. The Assembly Government should push for the devolution of powers for energy generation schemes over 50 MW and for the use of waste heat from power stations. (FoE Cymru 2011, 5)

However, this quotation also raises another problem, namely the difficulty for the Welsh institutions to reach their sustainable development targets, since the assessment of the NAW's energy policy so far is rather mixed.

Indeed, the NAW had committed to develop renewable energy in Wales, as stated in *Technical Advice Note 8*, mentioned earlier: 4 TWh of electricity per annum were to be produced by renewable energy by 2010 and 7 TWh by 2020 (WAG 2005, 3). Similarly, in *One Wales: One Planet* released in 2009, the WAG pledged to produce 20% of Wales's energy requirements from renewable sources: "Our aim is to generate annually more than 30 TWh of electricity from renewable sources by 2025 and 3 TWh of heat, mainly from biomass. Our aim is to produce more electricity from renewables than we consume as a nation within 20 years" (WAG 2009, 55). Wales currently consumes on average 24 TWh per year. Yet, this document remains quite vague, and no concrete proposals are made. As a result, we can question whether the WAG has reached the set targets.

In 2002, 2.4% of the electricity generated in Wales came from renewable sources, and this proportion increased to 5% in 2009, mainly thanks to increases in the proportion of wave, wind and solar power used. Half the energy, however, was generated by gas. These results were quite disappointing considering the very favorable conditions in the country for wind and marine energy production, as well as hydroelectricity, as indicated by Eilidh Johnston (ed.) in *The Welsh Potential for Renewable Energy*, the proceedings of a conference held (on September 19, 2002 in Llanberis) to explore the potential of renewable energy in bringing environmental, social and economic benefits to Wales. It was suggested that Wales had the potential to generate 20% of its energy from renewable sources by 2010. It may be wondered how the disappointing 5% produced can be explained.

The Welsh institutions have had to face problems with the production of renewable alternatives to traditional energy sources, especially when the Severn Barrage scheme, the centerpiece of the WAG's 2008 *Renewable Energy Route Map,* was dropped by the British government after a review concluded in 2010 that there was no strategic case for proceeding with the scheme at that time. The Severn Barrage was supposed to produce 9 TWh as a proportion of the 33 TWh of renewable electricity generation held in view by the WAG's route map as an aim for 2025. The cancellation of the project has left Wales more dependent on other sources of energy, most of them as controversial. The development of wind energy is also highly problematic, particularly when it comes to onshore schemes, which led the WAG to backtrack in 2011, thus yielding to the anti-wind lobby. Besides, there are two offshore schemes in Wales, one in the Bristol Channel and the other in the Irish Sea Zone, but they are unlikely to be built before 2016, their economic viability being not yet guaranteed. As a consequence, we may wonder what were the solutions left to the Welsh institutions, faced with so many obstacles. They could not possibly admit they were not allowed to decide, just as they were unable to promote nuclear energy. They had to adopt a pragmatic approach, so as to give the impression they preserved their authority and credibility.

As a result, the WAG launched an ambitious project, Energy Island Programme, in June 2010, when the British government announced it intended to build new nuclear reactors. It aimed to turn Anglesey into a major center of wind production and was to include a possible new nuclear station at Wylfa, along with offshore wind farm developments. It thus represents a huge scheme, with economic, social, and environmental benefits, since energy related projects could bring in up to 5,000 new jobs, while a further 2,500 could also be delivered by 2025 (BBC 2010). The building of a new nuclear station in Wales thus becomes included in a sustainable development initiative, respecting section 121 of the *GOWA 1998* and promoting an energy mix, as indicated in the description given by the Isle of Anglesey County Council on its website:

> Harnessing a rich mix of energy streams, including nuclear, wind, tidal, biomass, and solar; together with associated servicing projects provides major potential to achieve economic, social, and environmental gains for Anglesey and the wider North Wales region. (http://www.anglesey.gov.uk 2012)

The WAG's decision to support the building of a new reactor in Wylfa was part of this scheme, and thus easier to justify and defend. Since they had no choice, they obviously took advantage of the situation, but such a move may have alienated the support of the local population.

*

To conclude, this article has aimed to study how the British government used secrecy in order to prevent resistance from the Welsh periphery, but often to the detriment of democracy in the Principality. The NAW, set up in the late twentieth century, made considerable efforts to be transparent, in reaction to the previous history of Wales. And yet, as far as nuclear energy is concerned, the WAG has, in the end, resorted to the same secret practices, promoting a nuclear scheme after years of opposition to this type of energy. Such a u-turn reveals the pragmatism of the Welsh government, torn between theory and practice, that is to say between targets set in official documents and concrete obstacles. It is, nevertheless, in a very difficult position, as illustrated by the Environment Minister's contradictory declarations in early 2012. John Griffiths supported the building of new reactors on Anglesey on March 14, 2012, as indicated earlier, while calling for an all renewable energy electricity production 1 month later in an article entitled "Wales Should Ditch Nuclear Power, Says Environment Minister":

> Wales should match Scotland's ambition in aiming to generate all its energy from renewable energy and eventually ditch nuclear power, Wales' environment minister has said. [...] He also said it was his aim that nuclear sites in Wales—including the controversial Wylfa British site on Anglesey—should eventually be decommissioned, but insisted Welsh government support for a new reactor on Anglesey remained. (Henry 2012)

Can John Griffiths's deeply ambivalent position be explained by the announcement a few days before that Horizon's owners, RWE (Vorwe Gehen, one of Europe's five leading electricity and gas companies) and E.On (UK energy supplier and energy company), two German companies, were pulling out of the scheme for financial reasons? As revealed by this article, rumor had it then that he could be replaced as Environment Minister by Plaid Cymru AM Lord Dafydd Elis-Thomas, a rumor which he dismissed, considering that "there is all sorts of speculation in politics about all sorts of things, coalitions, changes in policy, reshuffles. That's the world we live in" (Henry 2012). He eventually remained in that post, but does this statement underline the fact that, in his view, we live in a system where state secrecy is only the necessary counterpart of inevitable speculation?

BIBLIOGRAPHY

ANON. 1957. "House of Lords." *Times*, March 14.

ANON. 1958. "Trawsfynydd." *Times*, February 17.

BBC. 2010. "Energy Island's Plan to Create Jobs on Anglesey." June 18. <http://bbc.co.uk> (accessed November 10, 2012).

Champenois, M. 2007. "À Cardiff, la démocratie en toute clarté." *Le Monde* 2, November 24.

Clews, R. 1980. *To Dream of Freedom. The Struggle of MAC and the Free Wales Army*. Talybont: Y Lolfa.

Clubb, G. 2012. Press release <http://foe.co.uk/cymru> (accessed November 10, 2012).

Friends of the Earth Cymru. 2001. "Another Windfarm Inquiry While Nuclear Waits for Fast Track Planning". Press release, December 3. http://foe.co.uk/cymru (accessed October 3, 2001).

Friends of the Earth Cymru. 2011. *Manifesto for a Greener Wales*. Cardiff: FoE Cymru.

Great Britain. 2003. *Our Energy Future—Creating a Low Carbon Economy*. Cmnd 5761. London: HMSO.

Henry, G. 2012. "Wales Should Ditch Nuclear Power, Says Environment Minister." April 16. <http://walesonline.co.uk> (accessed November 10, 2012).

Jenkins, L. J. "The Wind Power Debate." *Cambria*, 11, <http://www.cambriamagazine.com> (accessed March 10, 2006).

Kelsey, C. 2011. "From Nuclear Energy to Offshore Wind, Difficult Choices for Energy Planners." April 6. <http://walesonline.co.uk> (accessed November 10, 2012).

Kohr, L. 2012. *The Breakdown of Nations*. Routledge 1 Kegan Paul, 1957; repr. Totnes: Green Books.

Lawson (Lord). 1957. "Sites for Atomic Power Stations." House of Lords. *Times*, January 30.

Livingstone, T. 2008. "Nuclear Industry Must Pay to Deal with Waste." *Western Mail*, January 8.

National Assembly for Wales. 2000. *The National Assembly for Wales, The Essential Guide 2000*. Cardiff: The Stationery Office.

National Assembly for Wales. 2011. *The Legacy Report 2007–2011*. Cardiff: NAW.

National Assembly for Wales. <http://www.assemblywales.org> (accessed April 2, 2012).

Plaid Cymru. 2011. *Ambition is Critical. A Manifesto for a Better Wales*. Cardiff: Plaid Cymru.

Rawlings, R. (Prof). 2002. *Towards Parliament —Three Faces of the National Assembly for Wales*. Swansea: University of Wales.

Shipton, M. 2005a. "Secret Plan for Nuclear Power Plant." *Western Mail*, December 30.

Shipton, M. 2005b. "Minister 'Neutral' about New Nuclear Stations." *Western Mail*, December 31.

Welsh Assembly Government. 2005. *Technical Advice Note 8: Planning for Renewable Energy*. Cardiff: WAG.

Welsh Assembly Government. 2008. *Renewable Energy Route Map*. Cardiff: WAG.

Welsh Assembly Government. 2009. *One Wales: One Planet*. Cardiff: WAG.

Welsh Assembly Government. 2012. *Energy Wales: A Low Carbon Transition*. Cardiff: WAG.

Welsh Labour Party. 2011. *Standing Up for Wales*. Cardiff: Welsh Labour Party.

Wigley, D. 2001. *Maen i'r Wal*. Caernarfon: Gwasg Gwynedd.

Withers, M. 2006. "Is Wales Destined for a Nuclear Future?." *Wales on Sunday*, May 21.

CHAPTER 5

SECRETS, REVELATIONS, AND THE LIBERAL DEMOCRATS: A CASE STUDY IN BRITISH POLITICS

Muriel Cassel-Piccot
University Jean Moulin—Lyon III

In the modern age of democracy, instancy of communication has become the rule and political transparency has been on the ascent as evidenced by the passing of the Freedom of Information Act in the United Kingdom in 2000, its extension in 2012, and the WikiLeaks incidents[1] in 2010. In such a context, we may wonder whether "well-kept" secrets[2] in the upper reaches of power are conducive to the public good. Are they valuable agreements, beneficial to the community as a whole? Should they be reduced to the lowest possible number and achieve "best-kept"secret status? (Garton Ash 2011) Or on the contrary, should they consistently be broken and ideally be brought to public attention?

Implicitly promoting, improving and/or providing transparency in politics means seeking undistorted truth, grasping objective reality, acquiring comprehensive knowledge, avoiding contradictions, and finally gaining universal visibility. However, the process is obstructed when issues and elements are withheld and concealed from the people and reserved to a few insiders only. Thus the "outsiders", i.e. the citizens, are led to interpret kept-hidden or purposely omitted information as deception, fraud, dishonesty, opaqueness, and worse corruption. Such practices tend to generate, on the one hand, a disinterest in politics resulting in voter apathy and, on the other hand, populist views increasing the gap between politicians and electors.

Furthermore, secrecy is a paradoxical notion as it is meant to be discovered and only arouses interest once it has disappeared. Secrets are truly valuable

---

1 WikiLeaks is an international, online, non-profit organisation that publishes secret information. In 2010, it notably released documents about the Iraqi and Afghanistan wars and the U.S. State Department.
2 Secret, from Latin secretus, etymologically means set apart, withdrawn, hidden.

once they have been broken as significant new evidence and detailed explanations are added. Thus writing about political secrets is first and foremost writing about the inherent contradictions that lie at the heart of their failures and betrayals. Besides, the paradox contains ambiguities, as the ones who seek to maintain secrecy about facts and events have to reconcile remaining silent and communicating, adopting solutions and confronting new problems, forging links and provoking divisions, hiding treasures and bearing burdens, gaining freedom and enslaving themselves.

It is clear that transparency and secrecy are opposed notions even if, in practice, they do not exclude each other. In politics, defined as the conduct of the policy, actions and affairs of the state, the two concepts are closely associated with conflicts of interest, power games and fights for authority. This is the reason why the disclosures of political secrets are relished by the media but dreaded by politicians. At the national level, revelations have greater significance for a political group that has acquired third-party status and seeks to occupy a strong position on the political spectrum whether it is in the opposition or the junior partner in a coalition. The issue addressed here focuses on how the Liberal Democrats, whether they are the informers or the "betrayed", deal with the revelations of secrets. What is the nature of the disclosures? How are they dealt with? What impact do they have on the party and the party's image? Which social values do they convey? Which interpretations of the political stage do they give?

1. METHODOLOGY

The analysis will first present a synthesis of the various disclosed pieces of information involving the Liberal Democrat Party since its formation in 1988. It will look at how revelations are experienced, used, endured, and managed by the Liberal Democrat Party. More precisely it will focus on the nature of secrets, on informers, on how and why they are disclosed, and on the consequences they have. The following diagram summarizes results and organizes the analysis.

The square in the middle of the diagram stands for secrecy; the central square stands for secrets concerning the Liberal Democrats and the rectangle in the square represents secrets concerning other parties. The vertical axis shows the informers: in the upper half the Liberal Democrats, and in the lower part the "Non Liberal Democrats", i.e., political adversaries and

R E V E L A T I O N S

PROMOTION/
JUSTIFICATION

INCOHERENCE

DIFFERENTIATION

EFFICIENCY

PUBLIC

SPHERE

OPPORTUNISM/
MANIPULATION

LACK OF INTEGRITY

Ashdown/Campbell/
Laws
negotiations

Representatives
local issues

Davies/MEP/
Williams/Oakeshott
financial matters

Clegg/Laws
negotiations

L.D.
secret plans/notes

Rennard
impropriety

Clegg/Huhne
Opik/Cable
tensions

CORRUPTION

L.D.
MPS
expenses

FRAUD

Brown
campaign
2005

REVELATIONS BY LIB-DEMS

REVELATIONS BY NON LIB-DEMS

VISIBILITY

Clegg
smoking/
sexuality

Campbell
cancer

HONESTY/
TRANSPARENCY

Taylor/Kramer
cannabis

POLITICAL STAND

Kennedy
drinking

SECRETS

Clegg/
Huhne
wealth

LACK OF
COHERENCE

REJECTION

Oaten
prostitution

PRIVATE

SPHERE

Laws/Hughes
homosexuality

REJECTION

Clegg
family

Huhne
offence/lies

LACK OF

Ashdown/Huhne
adultery

RELIABILITY

IMMORALITY

R E V E L A T I O N S

Compiled by the author

97

the media or journalists, whose rights and duties "originate from the right of the public to be informed on events and opinions".[3] The horizontal axis shows the nature of the leaks. Indicated on the left hand-side of the diagram, they relate to the private sphere, including family history, private stories, and personal choices. Displayed on the right-hand side, they describe the public sphere, when politicians discuss and manage issues of national and international scopes. Each arrow in the graph stands for a secret that has been disclosed and points to a term written in bold and italics that considers the social impact of the secret when it is broken and brought to public attention. The dotted arrows stand for financial matters. On completion of the diagram with the major leaks that have occurred since the creation of the Liberal Democrat Party, two major lines of approach can be pursued. They correspond to the basic communication model focusing on the informers/senders of messages/major national players and the informed/receivers/voters.

2. Confidentiality, Privacy, and the Electorate

According to historian Antoine Prost, (Fournier 2003) British politicians who intend to carve out careers for themselves need to give evidence of irreproachable integrity as far as their private lives are concerned. Most notably in the 1990s, the uncovering of sex scandals in John Major's government described as "sleaze" in the British press led to the resignations of various ministers.[4] Today the social and cultural environment is saturated by the media, which with the advent of globalization and the development of information technology provide 24-hour news coverage. Moreover, they have developed a popular "celebrity culture", which has also pervaded the political stage and has enabled them to treat politicians harshly and disrespectfully (Kavanagh 2000). Indeed, the crossing of the boundary between political commitments and privacy has allowed the staging and dramatization of politicians' comings and goings whether they are shown as representatives of the people, husbands, fathers, sons, relatives, neighbors, or friends. This phenomenon provides means to draw audiences for the media and tools for politicians to win (or lose) voters. The former want

---

3   Declaration of the Rights and Duties of Journalists, Charter of Munich, 1971. The right to information, to freedom of expression and criticism is one of the fundamental rights of man.

4   Tim Yeo and Malcolm Sinclair under John Major.

to be seen, listened to, identified, recognized, and understood. Although exhibiting oneself on the public stage may be dangerous, it is also a way to show that, besides advocating and defending political positions, one experiences feelings, has desires, cultivates tastes, and gains experience. This type of exposure, i.e. public disclosure of private facts, occurs either in an apparently relaxed atmosphere with the adoption of a conversational tone when politicians wish to unveil their life[5] or in a climate of tension due to the pressure from the media which are keen to uncover scandals. In either case, the similarities (either real or imaginary) between the "governors" and the governed can be emphasized and used effectively (either positively or negatively) in particular during electoral campaigns.

In 2008, Nick Clegg gave an interview to Piers Morgan from GQ metrosexual magazine. He answered the journalist's questions straightforwardly when he talked about his youthful mistakes, his love affairs before he got married, and his relationships with his wife. Although he was criticized for being naive and lacking political skills, he managed to make himself noticed and make the third party heard after the Liberal Democrats' popularity had been decreasing under Menzies Campbell (*The Times* 2008) and only 4 months after his own election as leader. His parliamentary colleagues[6] took advantage of the situation to advertise their new head's open-mindedness and new style of politics. With time Nick Clegg has become more cautious but he keeps on insisting on his role as a normal man, a normal husband and a normal father. (*The NewStatesman* April 7, 2011) However, unlike Matthew Taylor and Susan Kramer, (*BBC* April 1, 2008) he has refused to say anything about smoking cannabis when he was young. It can fairly be argued that in an individual-oriented society, the exposure of a third party senior politician's private life contributes to the visibility, popularity, personification, and justifications of the organization. In other words, political and electoral legitimacy combines with media legitimacy. As it has long been argued and as Vince Cable quotes "Any publicity is better than none". (Cable 2009, 277)

On a traditionally adversarial political stage, the third party can be seen as a spoilsport. In this context, Liberal Democrats' personal lives have raised interest as they can be used as devices to show that the party is not a true party, that it is incapable of governing the country, and that it does not have a

---

5   S. Tisseron defines "extimité" as the opposite of privacy. Cf. *L'intimité surexposée* (Paris: Ramsay, 2001), 250.

6   Norman Lamb, Lembit Opik. Cf. http://news.bbc.co.uk./2/hi/uk_news/politics/7324541.smt (accessed May 7, 2013).

real purpose. There have been recurrent attempts at emphasizing the members' reputation as eccentrics ("Bearded men in sandals" (*BBC* September 25, 2002; (*Aulibdems* 2010) and "Granola eaters" (*The Economist* April 22, 2010), at demonstrating their lack of morality, and at pointing out inconsistencies between the party's values and its politicians' profiles. Chris Huhne was ironically nicknamed "Nine Homes Huhne", (*The Daily Telegraph* June 27, 2010) a criticism which hinted at the oversimplified contradiction between wealth and liberal democracy. His assets were thus questioned:

> The former cabinet minister, who earns tens of thousands of pounds a year from his considerable property portfolio, was also alleged to have engaged in questionable foreign exchange trading while an MEP (Member of the European Parliament). (*The Daily Telegraph* March 7, 2013)

As for Nick Clegg, he has been portrayed as a mock Conservative politician. (*ConservativeHome* 2008) If David Cameron's profile is fully in line with conservative ideology, Nick Clegg's has recurrently been presented as unfit for the Liberal Democrat Party. His ancestors, his family's possessions, and his relatives' occupations have been used against him: his grand-mother was a baroness; his Russian great-grand-aunt was a spy and Gorki's and H.G. Well's mistress; his Conservative father was a banker and a friend of Ken Clarke who has argued that "It would have been better if Nick Clegg had stuck with the political principles and wisdom of his father. Nick must regret sometimes having gone off into the strange wastelands of Liberal Democrat politics". (*BBC* April 21, 2010; *Channel4* April 21, 2010)

These comments call into question the roles and legitimacy of the two senior liberal democrats and bring discredit upon their moral values and ethical capabilities. They imply that they cannot really be trusted and that they cannot represent and embody "the fundamental values of liberty, equality and community" (*The Constitutions of the Liberal Democrats* 2012, Preamble) of the party. In this context, specific themes are used: apart from family background and wealth, there are also addictions (drugs, tobacco, and alcohol) and sexuality (homosexuality and extra-marital affairs).

Back to the early days of the Liberal Democrats, its first leader, charismatic Paddy Ashdown[7] was compelled to admit publicly that he had had an affair with his secretary, Tricia Howard, 5 years earlier. In late January 1992, he

---

7   Paddy Ashdown was the leader of the Liberal Democrats from 1988 until 1999.

was informed that the News of the World was about to break the story; he therefore took the decision to do it himself. In his Diaries, (Ashdown 2000, 132) he recalls the painful event step by step and in particular how he was nicknamed "Pantsdown" by The Sun (*The Sun* February 6, 1992). However, he concludes:

> And the British public at large seemed to be extraordinarily forgiving too—my opinion poll ratings actually went up as a result! I was in no doubt, though, that this did not mean that they approved of what I had done, only of the way it had been handled. So often in these matters it is the public lying that does the most damage. (Ashdown 2009, 258)

He also recurrently mentions the support of his wife Jane who behaved bravely, of front-bench colleagues, and of Prime Minister John Major. In more or less the same way but for different reasons, Simon Hughes[8] chose to apologize for not acknowledging that he was bisexual and as a result for being a hypocrite when he had accused his Labour adversary Peter Tatchell[9] of being a homosexual during the by-election of 1983. Just like Paddy Ashdown, he told the truth; the event caused him some harm, but he did not resign and even remained in the running for the 2006 leadership election although his campaign had been crippled (Cable 2009, 285). He did not become leader of the party but remained president from 2004 until 2008 and has been deputy leader since 2010.

Another aspect of politicians' personal lives that can affect their careers is addiction. In 2006, Charles Kennedy[10] was in a critical situation. His political career did not totally collapse at the time, but it has markedly declined since then. Speculations about his having a drink problem dated from September 2001. In 2004, he was urged by senior figures of the party to sort out his "health problem" and in 2005 criticisms were voiced about his leadership and poor performances in public. Finally, on January 6, 2006, Charles Ken-

---

8   Simon Hughes has been the MP for Bermondsey since 1983, today Bermondsey and Old Southwark. He has been the Deputy Leader of the Party since 2010. He has run unsuccessfully for the leadership of the party and for Mayor of London.

9   Peter Tatchell was a member of the Labour Party from 1978 until 2000; he joined the Green Party of England and Wales in 2004; he has been a political campaigner for the Lesbian, Gay, Bisexual and Transgender Movement since the 1990s.

10 Charles Kennedy has been an MP in the Highlands since 1983; he was Leader of the Liberal Democrats from 1999 until 2006.

nedy bowed to pressure from his own party's colleagues and to threat of information leakage by ITN.[11] (Cassel-Piccot 2006) Vince Cable remembers "Someone in the Shadow Cabinet leaked the contents (of the letter seeking Charles Kennedy's resignation) and I arrived back home to a media barrage on my doorstep" (Cable 2009, 284). As the secret could no longer be guarded for practical, political, and strategic reasons, it was broken. This logically led to the confession of the leader to his serious battle with alcoholism (*The Guardian* January 6, 2006) and finally to his resignation. He had received his wife's support; however, they divorced in December 2010 on the grounds of his "unreasonable behavior, according to papers released by the court". (*The Daily Telegraph* December 9, 2010) Charles Kennedy is still sitting in the House of Commons today; but he has definitely turned from a charismatic high-profile politician who led his party to its best national results (62 seats in the House of Commons in 2005) into a less eminent MP.

And yet Liberal Democrats who have undergone the same type of distressing experiences have not systematically been rescued after the disclosures of private secrets. On January 19, 2006, Mark Oaten, a young, promising and ambitious MP withdrew as a challenger for the leadership election for lack of support from his parliamentary party (*BBC* January 19, 2006). Three days later, he was forced to resign as Home Affair Spokesman in the Shadow Cabinet when the News of the World revealed that the married father of two children had had a relationship with a young male prostitute (Thurlbeck 2006). In 2010 election, Mark Oaten stood down from Parliament and retired from frontline politics after having published his memoirs (Oaten 2009). It should be added firstly, that Mark Oaten was "entangled in an embarrassing row over leaked emails" (*The Independent* January 19, 2006) concerning Charles Kennedy's support and secondly, that he later accused the media of releasing the information about the escort at a time when it would sell well, as they had known about the affair for 3 years (*Press Gazette* February 6, 2009). The scandal that ended Mark Oaten's political career clearly emphasizes crucial elements: when and how the secret is broken in relation to its potential impact on the audience.

Chris Huhne, who also contested the 2006 and 2010 leadership elections, is another preeminent Liberal Democrat who has failed to make a successful career in politics. Although he lost the second contest by a narrow mar-

---

11 Daisy McAndrew, Charles Kennedy's former spin doctor, was chief political correspondent for ITV News and thus working for ITN.

gin, he was a very influential MP who, in 2010, played a major role in the creation of the coalition and was appointed Secretary of State for Energy and Climate Change. In June of the same year he confirmed that he was leaving his wife Vicky Pryce for Carina Trimingham, (*The Guardian* June 20, 2010) a former BBC journalist who had helped him in his bid to become party leader, as the News of the World was going to publish their story. Once again, the newspaper had known about the extramarital relationship since 2009 but waited to bring it into the open until the right moment. At the time it had been suggested that Chris Huhne had possibly been targeted because he had demanded an inquiry into the News of the World phone-hacking scandal. (*The Guardian* June 20, 2010) Unlike Jane Ashdown—even though the situations were quite different—,[12] Vicky Pryce did not go quietly, filed for divorced immediately, and decided to make life extremely difficult for her former husband.

> In her quest to exact revenge, Pryce went to the press, telling Sunday Times political editor Isobel Oakeshott, she had information that if made public would destroy Huhne's political career. The allegations that someone close to Huhne had accepted speeding points on his behalf first appeared in the Sunday Times on May 8 2011(...). (*The Daily Telegraph* March 7, 2013)

Not only did the Energy Secretary ask his wife at the time to help him dodge the penalty back in 2003 but he also absolutely and consistently denied the speeding allegations and the charges for perverting the course of justice. He resigned as Energy Secretary in February 2012 when he learnt that he had to face criminal proceedings (*The Financial Times* February 3, 2012) and it was only in February 2013 that he decided to plead guilty after failing to have the case dismissed (*The Independent* February 5, 2013). He subsequently resigned as MP for Eastleigh and was sentenced to 8 month imprisonment but served only two (*BBC* May 13, 2013). Today the question remains whether his political career has been totally ruined or if it can be resumed in some way or other (*The Guardian* May 18, 2013). One thing is for sure, it has greatly been damaged and it has harmed the party now deprived of one of his most qualified experts and assets.

The analysis of the disclosures of secrets about senior Liberal Democrats' private lives points to several conclusions. Firstly, when secrets are revealed,

---

12 Paddy Ashdown, at the time Leader of the Liberal Democrats, had a brief affair with Tricia Howard while Chris Huhne left his wife for his lover.

attention is brought to the party, which enjoys much needed publicity on an adversarial stage. Secondly, upon disclosures, four items have to be taken into account: the timing of the exposure, in which the media play a significant role when they keep the news on hold; the nature of the hidden pieces of information, which can be rated according to their seriousness, from extramarital affairs to offences under the common law of England and Wales; the worsening of the situation by other instances of misconduct, questionable practices, and lies on the part of the politician; the trauma all the people involved suffer, including the party itself. Thirdly, the leaks produce two kinds of reactions on the part of the players involved that partly determine the outcome of the story: the strategy adopted, including lying, taking a step ahead of the media, admitting, explaining, and apologizing; the support or lack of it provided by the family and fellow-politicians, from compassion and understanding to desertion and career destruction. Fourthly, the end result can range from a simple mishap, which does not cause any severe impact on a political position, through gaining a back seat in politics to an exit from the arena of power. In other words, the British do not disregard politicians' personal lives, which are seen as closely linked to their public lives; conversely, British politicians, and especially the Liberal Democrats, should proceed with caution in this field. However, it should not be forgotten that they can also be undone by political scandals, by less acceptable hidden political behaviors and actions.

3. SECRECY, STRATEGY, AND POLITICS

Media attention is not only attracted by politicians' wealth and assets but also by their party's finances. During electoral campaigns, the Liberal Democrat Party's financial means are tight and cannot compare with the resources of the two main parties. However, between February 10 and March 30, 2005, it received a donation of 2,429,064 Pounds Sterling from Michael Brown, in addition to the 30,000 Pounds Sterling given for travel expenses (*The Guardian* April 10, 2011). On September 23, 2005, The Times published its investigations on the generous donor, a British businessman residing in Spain. The newspaper revealed his tumultuous past, and the existence of his company based in tax-heaven Switzerland (Zug). Convicted in his absence in November 2008 and sentenced to 7 years' imprisonment for theft, furnishing false information and perverting the course of justice, the fraudster remained nearly 4 years on the run before being finally brought before a British court in 2012. Although some victims believe that the Liberal Democrats should return the money because it is the proceeds of crime, (*The Guardian* April 22, 2012) the Electoral Commission has in the meantime confirmed that the Liberal Democrats were not guilty of any offence in accepting the sum in good faith (*BBC* May 1, 2012). However, this type of financial mismanagement can be damaging for the party, as it provides voters with reasons for questioning the integrity and honesty that the Liberal Democrats take pride in. In 2006 and 2007 however, the party avoided getting entangled in the "Cash for Honours"[13] scandal under Tony Blair's premiership.

In May 2009 though, they got involved in the MPs' expenses scandal like Labour and the Conservatives, but to a much lesser extent. The information was leaked by *The Daily Telegraph* (November 4, 2009), after failed attempts by Parliament to stop disclosure. The three major parties were concerned by the actual misuse of permitted allowances. Statistics showed that only 36% of Liberal Democrat MPs had to repay the government for undue payments against 51.6% for Labour MPs and 56.0% for Conservative MPs. The total amount of reimbursement per MP amounted to 2,330 Pounds Sterling for the Conservatives, 1,279 Pounds Sterling for Labour, and 681 Pounds Sterling for the Liberal Democrats (BBC). Data tend to prove that the Liberal Democrats are more principled and less venal than their counterparts; the episode was translated into a rise in popularity according to opinion surveys (*Politics* May 12, 2009). The positive image was darkened by the case of David Laws. After 18 days in government as Chief Secretary to the Treasury, he was forced to resign because he had illegally claimed expenses to pay rent for his partner. He paid back the 56,592 Pounds Sterling (*BBC* May 12, 2011) and apologized, explaining his "problems were caused by my desire to keep my sexuality secret" (*Politics* May 29, 2009). Because he was found to have made serious breaches of the rules by the Parliamentary Commissioner for Standards, he was also suspended from the House of Commons for a week in June 2011. After a period of 2 years, David Cameron decided to give one of the chief coalition negotiators, recognized for his expertise, a second chance. He brought him back to government as an Education Minister. It can fairly be argued that financial scandals have not really harmed the Liberal Democrats as they tend to adopt less deceitful behaviors than their Labour and Conservative counterparts. It should also be added that expertise and recognition are factors that can mitigate negative impacts.

---

13 The scandal concerned the offer of peerages in exchange for donations.

Other potentially damaging revelations relate to tensions within the party, internal rivalry and disagreements between members. As contenders in the leadership race, Nick Clegg and Chris Huhne were interviewed by Jon Sopel[14] on the live BBC Politics Show.[15] During the programme, the journalist showed Chris Huhne a document entitled Calamity Clegg, which had been written by his later discovered lover, Carina Trimingham. For different reasons both rivals were upset by the journalist's questions. The episode reflected the party's violent internal strife for power:

> In the Liberal Democrat leadership election of 2007, Chris Huhne's team cultivated doubts about his opponent's suitability for the job. "Calamity Clegg" was one particularly catchy moniker. The strategy almost succeeded: had it not been for delays to some postal votes, Mr. Huhne might have won. (*The Economist* February 9, 2013)

Despite the antagonistic performance, the two senior figures resumed their partnership and Chris Huhne was nominated Secretary of State for Energy and Climate Change. Moreover, when he decided to plead guilty and resigned as an MP in February 2013, Nick Clegg said that he was "shocked and saddened" (*The Guardian* February 4, 2013) In the end, the whole affair was not as damaging as it could have been:

> The public collapse of his (Huhne's) career (amid awful revelations of family discord) will not improve the public's already dismal opinion of politicians. But it does little damage to the Lib Dems, who count themselves lucky that they ended up with Calamity Clegg. Prior to his guilty plea, some had suggested that, if exonerated, Mr. Huhne ought to lead the party into the 2015 election. His leftish reputation endeared him to grassroots activists irked by their Conservative coalition partners (...) But Mr. Huhne's spectacular political demise has given Mr. Clegg, the devil they know, the healthy sheen of reliability. (*The Economist* February 9, 2013)

If Chris Huhne had won the leadership election, the party would have been in danger of irreparable damage. In addition, the outcome of the story

---

14 Jon Sopel is a BBC News presenter who hosted The Politics Show from 2005 until 2011. It was an hour long programme broadcast on Sundays.

15 Full transcript of the interview at http://news.bbc.co.uk/2/hi/programmes/politics_show/7093206.stm (accessed June 15, 2013).

proved Lembit Opik's harmful words about his new leader wrong; according to the WikiLeaks revelations published in December 2010, he had described Nick Clegg as "thick-skinned, avoiding direct confrontation" to the US ambassador Robert Tuttle. (*BBC* December 16, 2010)

Tensions within the party can be of a different type. In February 2013,[16] Lord Chris Rennard, the clever architect of Liberal rebirth from Paddy Ashdown to Nick Clegg, described as "a formidable and widely respected practitioner of political campaigning across all parties" (Ashdown 2000, 64) faced allegations of sexual misconduct:

> Women who worked for the Liberal Democrats have told Channel4 News that the party's most powerful official abused his position for years by inappropriately touching and propositioning them—and that leading Lib Dem MPs and peers who knew failed to take decisive action. The women say they complained about Lord Rennard, the Lib Dems' former chief executive, to senior party figures including the chief whip. But despite a manifesto commitment to equality, and tackling sex discrimination in the workplace, the party seemingly didn't do enough to root out sexual impropriety (...). (*Channel4* February 21, 2013)

The strain put on the party has been detrimental to its functioning and its popularity, which has decreased since its accession to power; its brand image has been smeared, all the more so as the person involved is seen as an achiever of success. US ambassador Robert Tuttle. (*BBC* December 16, 2010)

Tensions also emerged within the coalition at a time when differentiation was not yet on the agenda. In December 2010, Vincent Cable asserted, as he was taped by two undercover Daily Telegraph journalists,[17] that he had declared war to Rupert Murdoch, that being in the coalition was "like fighting a war, (*The Guardian* December 21, 2010; *The Daily Telegraph* December 20, 2010) and that he could bring the government down. As a consequence, he nearly lost his cabinet post as Business Secretary and was stripped of his responsibility for media policy over the BSkyB takeover involving Rupert Murdoch. (*The Guardian* December 21, 2010) Even if on May 10, 2011, the Press Complaints Commission ruled that the Daily Tele-

---

16 To make things worse, the news came out 2 weeks after Chris Huhne had taken responsibility for his misdeed.

17 Holly Watt and Laura Roberts.

graph had breached rules against the use of "subterfuge", the newspaper defended its action arguing that it had been in the public interest and that Liberal Democrat ministers "were not consistent in the private and public statements" about the coalition". (*Channel4* May 10, 2011)

In general, politicians are inclined to hide the daily internal workings of politics; they use secrecy as a means to an end, as a tool to conceal positions and strategies, which might otherwise be out of favor with their electors or might not bear fruit. For that purpose, some liberal democrat choices such as the legalization of cannabis or possible increases in VAT have not received publicity. The Liberal Democrats were the first party to officially favor the legalization of cannabis. The decision was voted during the 1994 conference to the disapproval of Paddy Ashdown and Alan Beith.[18] This position as a contributor to the permissive, overindulgent image of the party should not be voiced too loudly. The increase in VAT is another issue: officially the party was against but Vince Cable did not totally reject the idea and later justified the decision that was taken (*The LibDem Voice* June 23, 2010) In these two cases, the term "secret" might be an exaggeration; however, when the grassroots and the elite of the party do not agree, there is a tendency to hide the disagreements.

Remaining silent and secretive is also the rule when the Liberal Democrats need to negotiate with either the Labour or Conservative parties. During the 1992 general election campaign, Paddy Ashdown refused to say with whom he would ally in case of a hung Parliament but he had organized a conspiracy (Ashdown 2000***, 260) or negotiated ministerial posts with Neil Kinnock behind closed doors. More recently in 2010, Nick Clegg nominated a secret group of four members (Chris Huhne, Danny Alexander,[19] David Laws,[20] and Andrew Stunell[21]) whose mission was to prepare a potential coalition deal with the winner. Chris Huhne supported a strong partnership with the Conservatives, should they win the elections, while he publicly criticized them harshly, as he knew that the grassroots were particularly hostile to them. Similarly, the discourse on tuition fees was

---

18 Alan Beith has been the MP for Berwick Upon Tweed since 1973 and was deputy leader of the party from 1992 to 2002.

19 Danny Alexander has been the MP for Inverness, Nairn, Badenoch & Starthspey since 2005; he has been Chief Secretary to the Treasury since 2010.

20 David Laws has been the MP for Yeovil since 2001; he co-edited The Orange Book in 2004; he has been the Minister of State for Schools and the Cabinet Office since 2012.

21 Andrew Stunell is the MP for Hazel Grove since 1997.

quite different officially and informally. During the campaign Nick Clegg declared and even pledged that once in power he would abolish them while Danny Alexander wrote that the promise would and could not be kept in a confidential note dated March 16, 2010. Following the election on May 6, 2010, Conservative and Liberal Democrat negotiators were officially meeting to build up a coalition while links were privately established with the Labour Party. These examples prove that a third party in a two-party system, although modernized, has recourse to secrecy as a strategy to carve out a better place for themselves. This is how they can reach deals with the highest bidder and obtain the best possible results. Secrecy is also used to keep the party united, retain voters, and to avoid the dispersion of votes, i.e. to please the grassroots, focus on topical subjects as if anticipation were only reserved to the elite. This interpretation seems to favor a dual portrait of Liberal Democrat politics in which dialogues are distorted due to the specific position of the party and its struggle to remain in the forefront of government. Financial opaqueness, internal tensions between people and ideas at all levels of the party, and tactical negotiations appear to be necessary although dangerous. However, when ill-managed due to shortsightedness or misjudgment, they lead to disrepute and consequently a loss of popularity and votes.

Not only have the Liberal Democrats been subject to revelations, but they also have been informers themselves, using secret information as defensive and offensive weapons; they have voluntarily disclosed confidential news about themselves, their own party and the other parties. Indeed, they have been able to put forward their own ideological values by reporting irregularities performed by other organizations or institutions. In such a manner, they can prove that they are different from the others and emphasize their honesty and fairness. In 2003, councillor Alan Spratling made public a Conservative project aiming to sell off Emmbrook School, hinting at the pressure of property developers (*Wokingham LibDems* April 17, 2003). In 2007 and later in February 2011, Haringey Liberal Democrats exposed the Technopark regeneration failure, and unearthed figures showing the loss in revenue it implied. The revelation allowed them to blame the Labour Party for not acting in the interest of citizens. In 2009, Welsh Assembly Member Kirtsy Williams declared:

> In July, we uncovered evidence of questionable use of public
> money at IBW (International Business Wales) and raised con-

cerns about its performance. These reports justify our concerns in both areas. On performance, the report finds that IBW has not developed a strong brand, has failed to take advantage of opportunities from emerging economies like India and China and has left Wales at the bottom of the 12 UK regions when it comes to safeguarding jobs (...) On the issue of expenses, the report confirms our very worst fears about the culture of spending in IBW. (*KirstyWilliams* 2009)

In 2008 at the European level, Chris Davies uncovered the existence of the Gavin Report, an internal document about the systematic abuses of allowances by Euro MPs, which demonstrated fraud in staff costs on a massive scale. He refused to sign the confidentiality agreement and disclosed part of the report (*Observatoire des subventions* 2010; *The Sunday Times* February 22, 2009). At the national level, Lord Oakeshott, when he was a Liberal Democrat treasury spokesman in the House of Lords, compiled figures, denounced and condemned the bonuses pocketed by civil servants:

> Top civil servants get a very good salary averaging £1,500 a week and an excellent index-linked pension. Why do they need £200 a week extra just to get out of bed in the morning—more than many pensioners? (*LibDem Voice* June 17, 2009)

He later resigned from the frontbench over the issue of bank bonuses, as he dared to tell what he thought and criticized the government for not taking effective action (*The Guardian* February 9, 2011) With such pieces of information dealing with the central electoral themes of the economy and public finances, the Liberal Democrat Party strive to prove their efficiency, righteousness, and probity at the local, regional, national, and European levels.

The offensive strategy is coupled with a defensive one, often used when prominent politicians write their memoirs. Paddy Ashdown is unequivocal in his Diaries, when he relates his secret meetings with Tony Blair in detail most notably between 1993 and 1994. And indeed Menzies Campbell confirms the information:

> We (Ashdown et Blair) worked very closely together, co-ordinating our campaigns, including attacks on Major at Prime Minister's Questions, to a much greater extent than anyone has ever

realised (...) Paddy's private dealings with Blair even came to have a coded vocabulary of their own: "crossing the Rubicon" (...) Between 1994 and 1997, I was astonished the secret had been kept so well. (Campbell 2008, 131–132)

In insisting on their common viewpoints, Paddy Ashdown is able to set the record straight with a view to rehabilitating his party and his actions. It is a means to prove the party's role and value. Although Tony Blair confirms the first Liberal Democrat leader's words, he is more laconic:

Paddy, his wife Jane, Cherie and I dined together regularly before the election. We liked each other and trusted each other. Paddy had real leadership quality and like me was unafraid of taking on his party. (Blair 2010, 118)

For his part, Menzies Campbell relates how Gordon Brown got in touch with him with the utmost discretion in 2007 when he wanted to block the SNP before the election and when he was thinking of bringing Liberal Democrats in his cabinet (*The Guardian* June 20, 2007). Just like Paddy Ashdown before him, Menzies Campbell refused the offer; this is an episode which shows that promotion and development include the use of refusal skills. In a similar way, in his book 22 Days in May, David Laws insists on how secret affinity and sympathy can be shared by members of different parties and how they ease talks and actions at the highest level of the state.

In the public sphere, financial disclosures are not a bad point for the Liberal Democrats. They are rather safe as they appear to be less perverted than their counterparts and can return the argument against them to denounce a lack of probity. The second type of public revelations pertains to tensions, disagreements, and dissent at all levels: within the coalition, between senior members and between the elite and the grassroots. If fights and struggles are uncovered, expertise appears as a rescuer and protector. Finally, in order for a third party to win the battle of votes, strategy requires to be hidden.

*

On the political stage, secrets are common occurrences. Once they are on the verge of being leaked, they become embarrassing and potentially quite harmful. In a world in which the relationships between the elite and the masses have been changing, the disclosure of secrets and the handling of revelations have a great impact on politicians' lives and careers and on voters' opinions and behaviors. The main characteristic of these occurrences is that they are dual. They potentially offer visibility, familiarity, differentiation, efficiency, and promotion but at the same time they call into question integrity, reliability, probity, and coherence. They erode the stability and strength required for the exercise of power and expected by the electorate. In this context, three elements need to be taken into account and assessed: the power of the media which tend to push politicians into corners at precise moments of their choice; the strategies adopted by politicians to deal with the threat of disclosures or with revelations themselves; and finally the expertise, general behavior and profile of the politicians beside the revelations themselves. In a country where the dissociation between politician's private and public lives is difficult, the case study tends to demonstrate that when Liberal Democrats have been undone it was because of events in the private life rather than because of political mistakes or misjudgments. In this context, the ability to assess and anticipate events and to react promptly and to cultivate clear-sightedness are unquestionably great assets, which should be mastered. Although revelations contribute to the construction of British history, they exemplify a larger, more complex social reality in which apologies have become recurrent and accepted, even if, according to Vince Cable, "There are omissions too: secrets of the kind that all of us carry to the grave ". (Cable 2009, x)

BIBLIOGRAPHY

Ashdown, P. 2000. *The Ashdown Diaries: Volume One, 1988–1997*. London: Penguin.

Ashdown, P. 2009. *The Autobiography of Paddy Ashdown, A Fortunate Life*. London: Autumn Press Ltd.

Aulibdems. http://aulibdems.wordpress.com/2010/09/23/conference-a-round-up/ (accessed May 13, 2013).

BBC. http://news.bbc.co.uk/2/hi/uk_news/politics/2281017.stm. September 25, 2002 (accessed May 9, 2013).

BBC. http://news.bbc.co.uk/2/hi/uk_news/politics/4627798.stm. January 19, 2006 (accessed May 16, 2013).

BBC. http://news.bbc.co.uk/2/hi/uk_news/politics/7324541.stm. April 1, 2008 (accessed May 9, 2013).

*BBC.*http://news.bbc.co.uk/2/hi/uk_news/politics/election_ 2010/8634807.stm. April 21, 2010 (accessed May 13, 2013).

BBC. http://www.bbc.co.uk/news/uk-wales-12006416. December 16, 2010 (accessed June 15, 2013).

BBC. http://www.bbc.co.uk/news/uk-politics-13371746. May 12, 2011 (accessed June 16, 2013).

BBC. http://www.bbc.co.uk/news/uk-17911852. May 1, 2012 (accessed June 15, 2013).

BBC. http://www.bbc.co.uk/news/uk-22507000. May 13, 2013 (accessed June 15, 2013).

BBC. http://news.bbc.co.uk/2/hi/uk_news/politics/8493634.stm (accessed June 16, 2013).

Blair, T. 2010. *A Journey.* London: Hutchinson.

Cable, V. 2009. *Free Radical.* London: Atlantic Book.

Campbell, M. 2008. *My Autobiography.* London: Hodder and Stoughton.

Cassel-Piccot, M. 2006. "Choosing a Liberal Democrat Leader." International Symposium, Rennes, November 23.

*Channel4.*http://www.channel4.com/news/articles/vote_2010/ken% 2Bclarke%2Bnick%2Bclegg%2Bshould%2Bhave%2B been%2Ba%2Btory/3621502.html

Channel4. http://www.channel4.com/news/pcc-condemns-newspaper-over-vince-cable-tapes (accessed June 17, 2013).

Channel4. http://www.channel4.com/news/lib-dem-allegations-of-sexual -impropriety February 21, 2013 (accessed June 15, 2013).

ConservativeHome. http://conservativehome.blogs.com/centreright/2008 /04/nick-cleggs-tor.html (accessed June 15, 2013).

Fournier, E. 2003. "Hommes politiques : la mise en scène de la vie privée." *Sciences Humaines,* avril.

Garton Ash, T. 2011. "WikiLeaks has Altered the Leaking Game for Good. Secrets Must Be Fewer, but Better Kept." *The Guardian*, March 30.

Kavanagh, D. 2000. "Les politiciens face aux médias." In *Le Royaume-Uni de Tony Blair*. Pouvoirs n°93, avril.

KirstyWilliams. http://kirstywilliams.org.uk/en/article/2009/101694/ibw-reviews-demonstrate-serious-failings-in-government-s-approach-to-delivering-jobs-for-wales-welsh-lib-dems (accessed June 16, 2013).

LibDem Voice. http://www.libdemvoice.org/vince-cable-why-the-vat-rise-had-to-happen-20039.html

LibDem Voice. http://www.libdemvoice.org/lib-dems-reveal-civil-servants-paid-26m-in-bonuses-15396.html. June 23, 2010 (accessed June 17, 2013).

Oaten, M. 2009. *Screwing Up: How One MP Survived Politics, Scandal and Turning Forty*. Hull: Biteback.

Observatoire des subventions. http://www.observatoiredessubventions.com/2010/les-fraudes-des-deputes-europeens/ (accessed June 16, 2013).

Politics. http://www.politics.co.uk/news/2009/05/12/lib-dem-surge-following-expenses-scandal (accessed June 16, 2013).

Press Gazette. http://www.pressgazette.co.uk/node/43485. April 6, 2009 (accessed June 15, 2013).

The Daily Telegraph. 2010. "Chris Huhne: A Tale of Modern Manners." June 27.

The Daily Telegraph. 2010. "Charles Kennedy, Former Lib Dem Leader, Divorces Wife Sarah." December 9.

The Daily Telegraph. 2013. "Chris Huhne: The Role of Newspaper in Bringing him Down." March 7.

The Daily Telegraph. 2013. "'Dodgy Investments' Helped Chris Huhne Make Millions, Ex-wife Claims." March 7.

The Daily Telegraph. http://www.telegraph.co.uk/news/newstopics/mps-expenses/6499657/MPs-expenses-scandal-a-timeline.html. November 4, 2009 (accessed December 30, 2013).

The Daily Telegraph. http://www.telegraph.co.uk/news/politics/liberal democrats/8215501/Vince-Cable-transcript-of-his-meeting-with-reporters.html. December 20, 2010 (accessed June 16, 2013).

The Economist. 2013. "Nick Clegg, Comeback Kid?." February 9.

The Economist. http://www.economist.com/node/15954252. April 22, 2010 (accessed May 13, 2013).

The Financial Times. 2012. "Huhne Resigns as UK Energy Secretary." February 3.

The Guardian. 2010. "Chris Huhne Confirms He is Leaving his Wife." June 20.

The Guardian. 2011. "Lord Oakeshott Quits over George Osborne's Banking Deal." February 9.

The Guardian. http://www.guardian.co.uk/politics/2006/jan/06/uk.topstories3 (accessed June 17, 2013).

The Guardian. http://www.guardian.co.uk/olitics/2007/jun/20/uk.liberal democrats (accessed June 17, 2013).

The Guardian. http://www.guardian.co.uk/politics/2010/dec/21/vince-cable-could-end-coalition (accessed June 15, 2013).

The Guardian. http://www.guardian.co.uk/politics/2010/dec/21/vince-cable-war-murdoch-gaffe (accessed June 16, 2013).

The Guardian. http://www.guardian.co.uk/uk/2011/apr/10/conman-lib-dems-hiding-caribbean/print (accessed June 15, 2013).

The Guardian. http://www.guardian.co.uk/uk/2012/apr/22/lib-dem-donor-michael-brown-missing-millions (accessed June 15, 2013).

The Guardian. http://www.guardian.co.uk/uk/2013/feb/04/nick-clegg-chris-huhne-plea (accessed June 15, 2013).

The Guardian. http://www.guardian.co.uk/commentisfree/2013/may/18/should-chris-huhne-resume-political-life (accessed June 15, 2013).

The Independent. 2006. "Oaten to Quit Lib Dem Leadership Race." January 19.

The Independent. 2013. "Chris Huhne: A Political Career in Ruins, and all for Three Penalty Speeding Points." February 5.

The Liberal Democrats. 2012. *The Constitutions of the Liberal Democrats.* Preamble.

The NewStatesman. 2011. "I am not a Punchbag—I Have Feelings." Interview with Jemima Khan, April 7.

The Sun. 1992. "It's Paddy Pantsdown." February 6.

The Sunday Times. 2009. "Secret Report Reveals how MEPs make Millions." 22 February.

The Times. April 6, 1992.

The Times. 2008. "Lib Dem Leader Nick Clegg Keeps on Smiling Despite Torrid Week." May 5.

Thurlbeck, N. 2006. "Lib-Dem Oaten's 3-in-Bed-Rent-Boy Shame." *News of the World,* January 22.

*WokinghamLiberalDemocrats.*http://okinghamlibdems.org.uk/en/article/2003/120718/lib-dems-reveal-secret-tory-plans-to-sell-off-emmbrook-school. April 17, 2003 (accessed June 20, 2013).

CHAPTER 6

THE RIGHT TO REMAIN SILENT: ENGLISH POLICING AND THE CULTURE OF SECRECY

Emma Bell
University de Savoie, Chambéry

It has long been an established legal principle in the UK that individuals arrested by the police have a right to remain silent when questioned.[1] Yet in practice it is often the police themselves who behave as if they have a right to remain silent, cultivating a veritable culture of secrecy whereby the truth is manipulated in an attempt to protect the institution from public scandal. Despite recent attempts to improve police accountability and to give the public greater access to official information under the "freedom of information" legislation, the institution remains opaque, as has been revealed by a number of recent inquiries into the deaths of 96 football supporters at the Hillsborough Football Stadium and into the police killings of Jean Charles De Menezes, Ian Tomlinson, and Mark Duggan, not to mention investigations into the numerous deaths of citizens detained in police custody.

The term "culture of secrecy" is used in this chapter to refer to the idea that secrecy is built in to the institutional practice of policing in the UK, rather in the same way as Sir William Macpherson found that racism was "institutionalized", pervading "processes, attitudes, and behavior" throughout the police service, when heading his inquiry into the police investigation of the racist murder of black London teenager Stephen Lawrence in 1993 (MacPherson 1999). The term does not just refer to the attitudes of individual officers who are often reluctant to break a code of silence where this may open fellow officers to criticism, but also to the very practice of police work itself. Of course, the surveillance aspect of policing is necessarily carried out in secret with very little public transparency. Yet, there are many other aspects of police work which do not have to be shrouded in secrecy but which

---

1   It should be noted that this right is qualified: following Section 34 of the Criminal Justice and Public Order Act 1994, a defendant's decision to remain silent may in practice lead to an "adverse inference" being made by the prosecution.

nonetheless are. The idea of a *culture* of secrecy suggests that the police unthinkingly and reflexively engage in practices which entail the dissimulation of information and the spread of disinformation against the public interest.

This chapter seeks to outline a number of concrete examples of the way in which a culture of secrecy can impact upon police practice. It examines various failed attempts to improve police accountability, showing how difficult it is to dislodge this entrenched culture. It is argued that police officers, wittingly or not, adopt a culture of secrecy not simply to protect individual officers from prosecution but also to serve a particular political agenda which entails the enforcement of state control over certain populations to the exclusion of others, highlighting the criminal behavior of the powerless whilst diverting public attention from the extensive harms perpetrated by the powerful. Indeed, as Reiner (2000) underlines, policing must be understood as an inherently political action. The police help to construct a public narrative according to which the state and its institutions are justified in turning to authoritarian methods in order to provide physical security for the public at large. Current attempts on the part of the British state to "police the crisis" (Hall et al. 1978), whereby the public feel increasingly insecure despite a significant police presence, are regarded here as a desperate attempt to stem the tide of unrest and to seek legitimacy by scapegoating the most marginalized individuals for contemporary problems. Yet, the strategy risks being entirely counterproductive as the institutionalized corruption within British policing is revealed to the public, undermining trust and confidence and calling into question the extent to which the police are actually capable of shoring up the power of the neoliberal state. Nonetheless, a brief look at the direction in which policing may head in the future suggests that secrecy will remain institutionalized within the English police.

POLICE SECRECY/PUBLIC IGNORANCE

It is of course difficult to unearth the full extent of police secrecy. It takes many different forms, from the dissimulation of information, which may reflect badly on individual officers or on entire police forces, to the routine lack of transparency involved in everyday police work. At the time of writing (spring 2014), a Home Affairs Select Committee is continuing its long investigation into how undercover policing has been used in the UK following a series of revelations by *The Guardian* newspaper over the past 2 years. It has been alleged that a number of undercover police officers engaged in sexual relationships with women they were monitoring, in some cases fathering children. It was also revealed that undercover officers have been using the identities of deceased children. Scotland Yard has launched its own investigation into the controversy and there have been calls for a full public inquiry into undercover policing to be carried out.

This rather obvious example of police secrecy in practice is of particular note, not just because of the harm caused to members of the public involved, but also due to the fact that undercover policing is not only used to target known serious criminals but also peaceful environmental and political activists. Indeed, more generally, all forms of covert surveillance, while still focusing on serious crime, such as international terrorism, are increasingly used to target relatively minor illegal activity, such as simple car theft (Loftus and Goold 2012). A range of different kinds of surveillance may now be used by the police. The example highlighted above is known as Covert Human Intelligence and entails a police officer establishing a personal or professional relationship with a target in order to obtain information [ibid.]. But the police may also have recourse to intrusive surveillance, which may entail the monitoring of a private home or vehicle, and directed surveillance, aimed at gaining information for a specific operation without becoming intrusive.

The problem with these wide-ranging surveillance powers is that the safeguards normally accompanying overt policing practices are absent (even if the Regulation of Investigatory Powers Act 2000 attempted to provide some protections—see below). In addition, certain legal challenges to undercover policing operations, such as those brought by women claiming that their fundamental rights were breached when they were deceived into having an intimate relationship with undercover police officers[2], are to be heard in a secret court known as the Investigatory Powers Tribunal[3]. In this way, even investigations into police secrecy are themselves shrouded in secrecy.

---

2   AKJ and others v. Commissioner of Police for the Metropolis and others [2013] EWHC 32 (QB).

3   The Investigatory Powers Tribunal was established in 2000 to investigate complaints against public bodies concerning their relations with the public (notably over the use of surveillance by such bodies). The evidence put forward by the State remains secret and those who seek redress from the tribunal have no right of appeal or automatic right to an oral hearing. It should be noted that not all these legal challenges to the use of undercover policing are to be heard by the closed Investigatory Powers Tribunal. Claims for damages under common law are to be heard by the High Court, the usual place of redress for harms in civil law.

Yet, there have been a number of public investigations which have revealed the extent of a culture of police secrecy. Most recently, the Hillsborough Independent Panel, appointed in 2010 to look into the circumstances under which 96 football supporters were crushed to death at the Hillsborough football stadium in South Yorkshire in 1989, found that senior police officers deliberately sought to protect themselves from criticism of their handling of the tragedy by altering police statements (Hillsborough Independent Panel 2012). It was revealed that, following legal advice, police officers present on the ground as the catastrophe unfolded were not asked to fill in formal statements on Criminal Justice Act forms since their recollections were "not required for the purpose of any criminal investigation" (316). Instead, they simply jotted down their personal recollections of the events of that day which were then passed on to senior officers. At this stage, there was "an extensive process of review and alteration of the recollections and their transition to multi-purpose statements" (338) whereby statements considered to be "'unhelpful to the Force's case" were altered, deleted, or qualified (rewritten by the SYP team)'" (339). As one of the members of the Panel commented elsewhere, this "amounted to a systematic, institutionalized process of review and alteration intended to remove all criticisms of the police" (Scraton 2007, 67). This dissimulation of the truth was compounded by the refusal, until the appointment of the independent inquiry, of the authorities to grant access to primary statements and other evidence to the bereaved families. It took over 23 years for the truth to come to light; i.e. that, contrary to media and police reports, the Liverpool fans who died bore no responsibility for the tragedy which was instead caused by failings on the part of police, local stewards, and emergency services.

Many other tragedies, however, remain unsolved due to police secrecy. For example, no independent public inquiries have been held into the deaths of Jean-Charles de Menezes, Ian Tomlinson, or Mark Duggan[4] at the hands of the police, or into the deaths of scores of people in police custody. In 2011, the Independent Police Complaints Commission (IPCC)[5] estimated that over a 11-year period from 1998/99 to 2008/09, there were a total of 333 deaths in or following police custody. These are defined as follows:

---

4   These cases represent just a few examples. Other highly-publicized killings by police officers have included Kevin Gately, Blair Peach, Richard O'Brien, Shiji Lapite, Roger Sylvester, Harry Stanley, and Mikey Powell.

5   The IPCC is discussed below. See p. 7.

... deaths of persons who have been arrested or otherwise detained by the police. It includes deaths which occur whilst a
person is being arrested or taken into detention. The death may
have taken place on police, private or medical premises, in a public place or in a police or other vehicles. (IPCC 2009, 3, cited by
IPCC 2012)

These figures were criticized (see, for example, Stickler, Bell, and Mole
2012; Stickler 2012) for not having included those who were never arrested or detained by the police but who nonetheless died during or following
police contact. An investigation for *The Independent* newspaper and The
Bureau of Investigative Journalism found that a number of high-profile
cases were not included in the statistics (Stickler 2012). This led to the
government's chief statistician producing a report on the IPCC statistics. It
found that whilst "some confusion may have been caused" by not including
these particular cases, there was "no evidence ... that cases that should have
been included in either publication have not been" (Government Statistical Service 2012, 8). According to INQUEST, over approximately the same
period as that covered by the IPCC (1998–2008), there were 476 deaths in
police custody in England and Wales and additional 32 people shot by the
police and 343 deaths in police pursuits and road traffic incidents involving
the police (Inquest 2013). The huge disparity between these two sets of
figures suggests reluctance on the part of the police and the official agencies
charged with monitoring police actions to reveal the true extent of deaths
in police custody.

There has been a similar reluctance to publicly discuss a number of high-profile police shooting incidents. De Menezes, aged just 27, was shot seven
times at point blank range by special firearms officers from the London
Metropolitan Police at Stockwell tube station in London in July 2005. The
officers had been trained to shoot potential suicide bombers in the head
as part of an anti-terrorist shoot-to-kill policy known as Operation Kratos.
They believed that De Menezes was planning to detonate an explosive de-
vice in the London Underground. Yet, despite reports by the Metropolitan
Police Authority[6] (MPA 2008), two inquiries by the IPCC (IPCC 2007a,
2007b) and three court trials,[7] the circumstances in which De Menezes was

---

6   The MPA is the independent monitoring board for the London Metropolitan Police.
7   The Crown Prosecution Service's decision not to bring charges against individual offi-
    cers was successfully challenged in an administrative court (see R (on the application

killed have still not been made clear to the public. Central to this lack of disclosure has been the refusal on the part of the police to openly discuss its counter-terror strategy. Indeed, they have consistently refused to admit that De Menezes was killed under Operation Kratos in order to avoid such public discussion (Smith 2012).

The case of Ian Tomlinson, a newspaper vendor who collapsed and died after being struck by a police officer on his way home from work during the G20 protests in 2009, is a clear example of police denial and dissimulation of the truth. Immediately after Tomlinson's death, the Metropolitan Police issued a public statement denying that its officers had had any contact with its officers prior to his collapse. It was only 4 days later that video footage handed over to the press by a member of the public revealed what had really happened: a Territorial Support Group[8] officer, Simon Harwood, had struck and pushed Tomlinson immediately before he fell to the ground. In addition, it was later found that the Home Office-appointed pathologist, Freddy Patel, had failed to examine the possibility that Harwood's actions could have led to Tomlinson's death, instead attributing it to cardiac arrest. Harwood was later tried and found not guilty for manslaughter, although he was subject to a disciplinary hearing and sacked for gross misconduct. What was interesting about this case was that the public and the news media were able to lift the veil of secrecy over police practice (Greer and McLaughlin 2012).

Where inquiries have taken place, such as that into the police shooting of Azelle Rodney in Edgware, London, in 2005,[9] they have been delayed for years due to police and government resistance to hand over evidence relating to intercepted communications obtained during undercover policing operations. Rodney was shot six times at point-blank range by an unnamed police officer (known only as E7) in the course of a drugs-related policing operation. His family hopes that the inquiry will be able to determine exactly why the officer concerned believed this course of action to be necessary.

---

of da Silva) v DPP [2006] EWHC 3204 Admin); the Metropolitan Police was successfully prosecuted for breach of the Health and Safety at Work Act 1974 by failing to provide for De Menezes' health, safety and welfare; a coroner's inquest jury found that the killing had been lawful.

8   The Territorial Support Group is a specially-trained police unit trained in dealing with public order and terrorist threats.

9   The inquiry's findings are due to be published in the course of 2013.

The family of Mark Duggan, the black man shot by the police in Totten-ham, London, in August 2011, sparking riots across English cities, is hav-ing similar difficulties establishing the circumstances of his death. A formal inquest began in September 2013, more than 2 years after the incident, but evidence provided by firearms officers has remained secret. The inquest re-ported in January 2014, concluding that Duggan has been lawfully shot, de-spite being unarmed. The IPCC, which continues its long investigation into the shooting of Mark Duggan, described this inability to disclose certain forms of police evidence, such as that gathered by the police during phone intercepts, as a hindrance to its own inquiry. In March 2012, it issued a for-mal statement declaring:

> Our principal statutory duty is to secure and maintain confi-dence in the police complaints system and one way in which this can be achieved is by ensuring that there is proper public scrutiny when someone dies at the hands of the state. We are therefore extremely frustrated when anyone or anything at-tempts to get in the way of our ability to provide family mem-bers with information about an investigation into a death at the hands of the police or to ensure a full public examination of the facts surrounding the death. As a general rule we seek to find ways round any such obstacles. However, in some circumstanc-es our hands are tied by the law. One such provision is s.17 of the Regulation of Investigatory Powers Act 2000. The impact of this is that not only can some information not be disclosed; we cannot even explain why we cannot disclose the information, as this itself would be a breach of the law. In our view this places investigatory bodies in the invidious position of being unable to provide families, and the public, with meaningful informa-tion on the investigation or even explain why that information cannot be provided. We believe this law needs to be changed. (IPCC 2012)

In many cases, therefore, police secrecy is actually protected by the legal system. Yet, in recent years there have also been attempts to use the legal system to improve accountability which should in theory allow the public greater access to information held by the police.

POLICE ACCOUNTABILITY: LIFTING THE VEIL OF SECRECY?

Efforts to improve police transparency are not entirely new. Already in the early post-war period, the Commissioner of the Metropolitan Police, Sir Harold Scott, alluded to the atmosphere of secrecy in Scotland Yard and thus sought to improve press and public relations to "give the fullest and earliest information to the press on police activities" (Scott 1954, 92, cited by Mawby 2002, 306). This trend continued in the 1970s and through to the contemporary period, yet the policy of openness was counterbalanced by one of control of information. For example, while journalists were briefed more openly, they were forced to carry "Press Identification Cards" which were issued at the discretion of the Metropolitan Police (Mawby 2002).

There has also been a series of legislative attempts to improve police accountability. In 1984 the Police and Criminal Evidence Act (PACE) counterbalanced a significant increase in police powers (notably greater stop and search powers) with the introduction of a number of safeguards intended to improve police accountability. For example, it was at this time that the obligation on the police to contemporaneously record interviews was introduced (see Reiner 2000, 176–183). Yet, while the Act forced police officers to comply with strictly drawn-up rules, breach of which can lead to serious disciplinary proceedings, it did little to change the overall culture of the police (182–183).

In 1998 the Human Rights Act (HRA) placed an obligation on police officers to ensure that their practices do not infringe fundamental rights as outlined in the Act. Yet, it would seem that the Act has failed in its aim to create a "human rights culture" since although officers are now more aware of human rights issues, they have not fundamentally changed the way they operate. Indeed, compliance with tests laid down by the HRA serves to legitimize existing police actions. Relying on extensive field research, Bullock and Johnson found that the qualifications outlined in the Act were viewed as "sufficient to give the police the powers that they need to do their job" (officer cited by Bullock and Johnson 2012, 643). While the HRA has increased police bureaucracy by obliging officers to keep reports in compliance with the Act, it has failed in practice to offer any direct challenge to the prevailing culture of secrecy.

In 2000 the Freedom of Information Act (FOIA) was passed, granting members of the public access to information held about them by public bodies, including the police. However, there are serious limits to the kinds of information which may be disclosed. The FOIA provides a wide exemption for information which pertains to a criminal investigation, provided that the public interest in preventing the release of information outweighs the public interest in obtaining it. Even once a criminal investigation is closed, the release of information pertaining to it continues to be blocked despite the recommendations of the Macpherson Report (Fisher 1999, 20).

Rather like PACE, the Regulation of Investigatory Powers Act 2000 (RIPA) sought to balance increased police surveillance powers with increased regulation of those same powers. All powers are to be used in a way that is "necessary, proportionate, and compatible with human rights". Yet, in practice the balance of power under RIPA would appear to be very much in favor of the police. Under the Act, the police may, for example, demand data from telephone companies in respect of an account or an individual, and engage in covert surveillance operations themselves, intercepting communications, conducting covert surveillance, and accessing encrypted electronic data. The Act has been relied on to prevent information sourced in such a way from being made public. Hence, the trials involving undercover surveillance operators cited above are to be held in secret. Some intercepted evidence cannot even be revealed in legal proceedings such as inquests. As mentioned above, this has hindered the IPCC investigation into the shooting of Mark Duggan. It also led to the inquest into the death of Azelle Rodney being abandoned.

Perhaps the greatest problem when it comes to police accountability is that bodies intended to open the police up to external scrutiny lack teeth. The Independent Police Complaints Commission (IPCC), created following the Police Reform Act of 2002, replaced the previous police complaints authority. The IPCC is meant to be an entirely independent body, investigating complaints and allegations of misconduct against the police in England and Wales. Yet, as highlighted above, it faces similar problems to any member of the public when it comes to gaining access to sensitive police records. In addition, it is only meant to investigate a small number of complaints, with the rest being dealt with by the ordinary police complaints departments—indeed, it was estimated in 2010 that the IPCC investigates less than 1% of all complaints against the police (Savage 2013, 98). Perhaps even more problematic is the fact that the body is liable to "regulatory capture" meaning that those charged with regulation are likely to be too close to the police and largely dependent on police support (109).

There is often a feeling among members of the public that the police benefit from a certain impunity. Indeed, the officer responsible for the death of Ian Tomlinson, although he was eventually tried for manslaughter, was found not guilty. In his evidence to a Home Affairs Committee on the impact of the Macpherson Report 10 years on, Duwayne Brooks, Liberal Democrat MP and friend of the murdered Stephen Lawrence lamented the fact that no police officer has been successfully prosecuted for deaths such as Tomlinson's over the past 15 years and worried that officers "feel that they are above the law and can behave as so. Until the same employment and criminal procedures are brought to bear on them that are brought to bear on the rest of us, the real problems of police unlawfulness, whether it be racism or assaults will remain unchecked" (Brooks, cited in House of Commons 2009, 29). Indeed, while police officers feel that their secrets are protected by laws such as RIPA, there is a danger that they may appear to be above the law, harming their legitimacy before the public.

POLICING THE CRISIS

Even though it threatens to undermine police legitimacy, protecting a culture of secrecy within the police force can also be a way of preserving the myth of consensual policing whereby the police do no more than is necessary to protect the public from crime, assuming a "scarecrow function", preventing crime largely via the presence of uniformed officers on the beat (Reiner 2000, 76). Preventing the public from discovering the extent of police surveillance is perhaps one way of shoring up the myth of the "British bobby" as an essentially benign force.

Yet, the police do not merely act to protect individual officers from prosecution or the police as an institution from shame. Whether intentionally or not, they serve a particular political agenda, justifying the state's authoritarian actions against certain populations who are regarded as troublesome or threatening: suspected terrorists such as Jean-Charles de Menezes; black youths like Azelle Rodney or Mark Duggan thought to be involved in drug dealing; protesters or those simply caught up in protests like Ian Tomlinson; rowdy members of the working class, such as the Liverpool supporters at Hillsborough football grounds ... The protection of police secrecy allows the police and the state, often assisted by the media, to continue to depict these groups as problematic and the institutions of the state as virtuous. Indeed, it was only once the veil of secrecy had been lifted over these particular events that it became clear to what extent the police initially misrepresented the victims of their own professional errors in an attempt to justify their actions.

The demonization of the social groups who normally bear the brunt of police power, those who Reiner describes as "police property" (Reiner 2000), enables the State to find suitable scapegoats for contemporary social problems, thus diverting attention away from its own powerlessness to prevent these same problems, be they social exclusion or terrorist attacks. Meanwhile, the public gaze is directed downwards, to those at the margins of society, rather than to the corruption which exists at the top.

Yet, such a strategy risks seriously undermining police legitimacy since, as Reiner points out, this is secured only when "those at the sharp end of police practices do not extend their resentment at specific actions into a generalised withdrawal of legitimacy from the institution of policing *per se*" (Reiner 2000, 49). This is precisely what is occurring, especially when specific actions, such as the killing of Mark Duggan, can be seen as part of a wider trend towards the police victimization of minority groups (black people, for example, are seven times more likely than white people to be stopped and searched by the police—Ministry of Justice 2010, 26). Furthermore, resentment of the police has spread beyond "those at the sharp end", increasingly involving the middle classes who have themselves borne the brunt of authoritarian policing tactics such as kettling when attending public demonstrations. Blatant injustices and blunders such as the shooting of the innocent De Menezes also risk undermining middle class support for the police. We noted above how it was the largely middle class media which bought the real circumstances of Ian Tomlinson's death to light, thus undermining the official version of the incident.

The state's response has been piecemeal reform on the one hand (such as the creation of the IPCC) and a desperate attempt to protect police practices from public scrutiny on the other (via RIPA, for example). This suggests that secrecy is likely to remain institutionalized with the English police and the state on which it depends, regardless of attempts to give the police force a democratic gloss. It is essential for the state that the police continue to police the crisis (Hall et al. 1978), diverting attention from its failure to provide either physical or economic security to its citizenry.

The Future of Policing:
from Accountability to Populism

In order to confer legitimacy upon what is now an increasingly contested institution (Reiner 2000), we have seen how recent reforms have attempted to make the English police more accountable to the public. Yet, a number of contemporaneous trends risk further blurring the lines of accountability. For example, the contracting out of some core police functions to the private sector may add yet more layers of secrecy to an already obscure institution. In March 2012, *The Guardian* revealed plans by West Midlands and Surrey police to hand the delivery of a wide range of services, such as patrolling the streets and detaining suspects, to the private sector (*The Guardian* 2012). O'Reilly and Ellison suggest that where the state uses the police to protect its own agenda, private companies providing security services will similarly seek to protect their own corporate interests, thus leading to an extension of what they describe as a "secrecy complex" whereby the web of secrecy is reinforced by public and private actors (O'Reilly and Ellison 2006, 649).

More generally, the introduction of market principles into police services has placed immense pressure on the police to meet measurable performance-based targets, something which may oblige the police to cut corners or conceal errors which may prevent them from fulfilling such targets. Furthermore, accountability is not just to be shared with the private sector but also with the European Union, as joint security agreements are signed regarding international organized crime and terrorism, for example, further jeopardizing police transparency vis-a-vis the public. Even reforms which may appear to be extremely democratic on the surface, intended to allow the public to hold the police to account, are unlikely to make the police more accountable. For example, recently elected Police and Crime Commissioners (PCCs)[10] may lead instead to further politicization if they are tempted to adopt populist policies and interfere in the running of local police forces.

Furthermore, it is hard to challenge the culture of secrecy within the police at a time when the government is seeking to extend such a culture within the legal system as a whole. Under the new Justice and Security Act, passed

---

10 The first PCCs were elected across England and Wales in November 2012. They have powers to appoint the local chief constable and ostensibly to hold police forces to account.

in 2013, secret court hearings may become a default measure, used not as a last resort, but as a routine practice when civil cases involve national security issues. The government may legitimately defend serious allegations against itself and its agents (such as serious violations of human rights) without ever having to reveal secret material to the claimant, the public or the press, thus exacerbating the problems of police secrecy highlighted above. Police secrecy may thus be regarded as just one aspect of a wider culture of secrecy entrenched in the state itself.

BIBLIOGRAPHY

Bullock, K., and P. Johnson. 2012. "The Impact of the Human Rights Act 1998 on Policing in England and Wales." *British Journal of Criminology* 52: 630–650.

Fisher, M. 1999. "Keeping Shtum." *Index on Censorship* 28: 19–23.

Greer, C., and E. McLaughlin. 2012. "'This is not Justice': Ian Tomlinson, Institutional Failure and the Press Politics of Outrage." *British Journal of Criminology* 52 (2): 274–293.

Government Statistical Service. 2012. *National Statistician's Review of IPCC Statistics on Deaths During or Following Police Contact.* http://www.statisticsauthority.gov.uk/national-statistician/ns-reports--reviews-and-guidance/national-statistician-s-reviews/national-statistician-s-review-of-ipcc-statistics.html (accessed April 25, 2014).

Hall, S. et al. 1978. *Policing the Crisis: Mugging, The State, and Law and Order.* London: Macmillan.

Hillsborough Independent Panel. *Permanent Archive for the Hillsborough Disaster.* http://hillsborough.independent.gov.uk/report/main-section/part-3/ (accessed April 25, 2014).

Hillsborough Independent Panel. 2012. *Hillsborough.* London: HMSO.

House of Commons. 2009. *House of Commons Home Affairs Committee: The Macpherson Report—Ten Years On.* London, HMSO.

Inquest. *Deaths in Police Custody.* http://www.inquest.org.uk/ [accessed February 22, 2013).

IPCC. 2007a. *Stockwell One: Investigation into the Shooting of Jean Charles de Menezes at Stockwell Underground Station on 22 July 2005.* http://www.ipcc. gov.uk/Documents/stockwell_one.pdf (accessed April 22, 2014).

IPCC. 2007b. *Stockwell Two: An Investigation into Complaints about the Metropolitan Police Service's Handling of Public Statements Following the Shooting of Jean Charles de Menezes on 22 July 2005.* http://www.ipcc. gov.uk/Documents /ipcc_stockwell_2.pdf (accessed April 22, 2014).

IPCC. 2011. *Deaths in or Following Police Custody: An Examination of the Cases 1998/99–2008/09.* http://www.ipcc.gov.uk/en/Pages/ deathscustodystudy.as px (accessed April 25, 2014).

IPCC.*RIPA Statement for IPCC Deputy Chair Deborah Glass.*http://www.ipcc. gov.uk/news/Pages/pr290312_ripa_statement.aspx [accessed February 11, 2013).

Loftus, B., and B. Goold. 2011. "Covert Surveillance and the Invisibilities of Policing." *Criminology and Criminal Justice* 12 (3): 275–288.

MacPherson, W. 1999. *The Stephen Lawrence Inquiry*, Cm 4262-I. London: Home Office.

Mawby, R. 2002. "Continuity and Change, Convergence and Divergence: The Policy and Practice of Police—Media Relations." *Criminology and Criminal Justice* 2 (3): 303–324.

Ministry of Justice. 2010. *Statistics on Race and the Criminal Justice System 2008/09.* London: HMSO.

MPA. 2008. *Stockwell Scrutiny.* http://policeauthority.org/metropolitan/ scrutinies/stockwell/index.html (accessed February 11, 2013).

O'Reilly, C., and G. Ellison. 2008. "Eye Spy Private High: Re-Conceptualising High Policing Theory." *British Journal of Criminology* 46: 641–660.

Reiner, R. 2000. *The Politics of the Police.* Oxford: OUP.

Savage, S. 2013. "Thinking Independence: Calling the Police to Account Through the Independent Investigation of Police Complaints." *British Journal of Criminology* 53: 94–112.

Smith, G. 2012. "Shoot-to-kill Counter-suicide Terrorism: Anatomy of Un-democratic Policing." In *Counter-Terrorism and State Political Violence: The 'War on Terror' as Terror,* eds. S. Poynting and D. Whyte. Oxon: Routledge.

Stickler, A. 2012. "How Many Have Died After Police Restraint? MP Calls for Inquiry." *Bureau of Investigative Journalism,* January 31.

Stickler, A., D. Bell, and C. Mole. 2012. "Rate of Deaths in Custody is Higher than Officials Admit." *The Independent,* January 31.

The Guardian. 2012. "Key Extract of Contract Note for Bidders for Police Services." March 2. http://www.guardian.co.uk/uk/interactive/2012/mar/02/contract-note-bidders-police-services (accessed April 25, 2014).

CHAPTER 7

SECRECY AND JUSTICE: THE ENGLISH EXAMPLE OF LEGAL PROFESSIONAL PRIVILEGE

Marion Charret-Del Bove
University Jean Moulin—Lyon 3

In most developed legal systems, special protection is granted to communication between lawyers and clients. As a matter of fact, "strict confidentiality" is the notion that best encapsulates the nature of a lawyer's work, especially in criminal cases where it is often said that the prohibition on breach of confidence is nearly absolute. As stated by David Luban in *Lawyers and Justice*: "The duty of confidentiality makes lawyers special; it is a code of silence that seals their lips in a way that other employees' lips are not sealed" (180). What is true for American attorneys proves to be as true for English barristers and solicitors. The leitmotiv of secrecy punctuates English case law such as in *R v. Derby Magistrates' Court, ex parte B* where Lord Taylor of Gosforth argued that "the mouth of such a person [a lawyer] is shut forever" (para 47). Just as every reasonable person owes their neighbors a duty of care, so every lawyer owes their clients a duty of confidentiality. In the case just mentioned Lord Taylor related a brief history of the privilege going as far back as the late sixteenth century, and evoked a series of cases—*Berd v. Lovelace* in 1577, *Dennis v. Codrington* in 1579 cited in *R v. Derby* paras 42 and 44—where solicitors, who had acted as counsel in the matters involved, were not compelled to testify.

Secrecy within a legal and professional context has long been legitimized and is called legal professional privilege (LPP) in England and Wales, attorney–client privilege in the USA. It currently provides that all communications between a legal adviser and their clients are protected from disclosure. However, secrets are negatively perceived. They are associated with deception and disloyalty; they reek of lies and deceit, two words at odds with transparency and the way current English civil cases should be currently handled following the adoption of new Civil Procedure Rules

(CPR) in 1998 with the "overriding objective of enabling the court to deal with cases justly" [Rule 1.1(1)].

Thus, disclosure is one keyword of the English adversarial justice system that ensures that the parties to a dispute—be it criminal or civil—are entitled to fair and equal treatment. It guarantees that the party to whom a document has been disclosed—i.e. when the party is informed of its existence—has the right to inspect that document. Indeed, Gary Slapper and David Kelly focus on the idea of cooperation between parties in the course of litigation: "parties are encouraged to cooperate with each other in the conduct of proceedings" (278). The authors explain how parties are also constantly reminded of the need for cooperation through official statements of interpretative guidance called practice directions (280). As a consequence, the parties to a case are supposedly on an equal footing, all of them playing with their cards on the table.

This article aims at explaining the existence and persistence of secrecy in a legal context, within the framework of a procedure based on transparency and disclosure. Is it possible to reconcile the necessarily uninhibited private communication between lawyer and client with the principle of full disclosure vital for the courts to decide properly and ensure fair justice? Before answering such a tricky question, it seems relevant to start with a definition of LPP as it is asserted in England and Wales.

1. Definitions

Even though there is no statutory source defining LPP—the concept being derived from case law—it was early stated in a significant case, *Greenough v Gaskell* [1833], where the Lord Chancellor ruled that:

> In all such cases, it is plain that the attorney is not called upon to disclose matters which he can be said to have learned by communication with his client or on his client's behalf, matters which were so committed to him in his capacity of attorney, and matters which in that capacity alone he had come to know. (104–105)

In this case, the defendant, a solicitor called Gaskell, was accused of fraud by the plaintiffs who claimed Gaskell had concealed his client's insolvency, Mr. Darwell, and had falsely represented his client's difficulties as being temporary only, despite Gaskell's knowledge of the situation. For his defence, Gaskell argued that even if he was aware of his client's financial situation at the time of the transaction, all the relevant documents in his possession related to his client's insolvency were received by him while being professionally employed in his capacity as solicitor for his client, and were thus privileged. This case early determined that LPP was attached to the communications that took place between someone and a legally consulted lawyer.

There are in fact two forms of LPP, legal advice privilege (LAP) and litigation privilege (LP).

> The modern case law on legal professional privilege has divided the privilege into two categories, legal advice privilege and litigation privilege. Litigation privilege covers all documents brought into being for the purposes of litigation. Legal advice privilege covers communications between lawyers and their clients whereby legal advice is sought or given. (*Three Rivers No 6*: para 10)

In both situations, immunity from compulsory disclosure is granted to all privileged, i.e. confidential communications. It is first and foremost necessary to stress the slight difference there is between "confidential" and "privileged". The former is a synonym with secret and refers to written or oral communication between a lawyer and his client. The latter is the adjective employed to describe confidential information allowed to remain secret. Thus, only confidential communications are covered by LPP. Such documents and material attract protection from disclosure because of the ethical duty of confidentiality a lawyer owes his client even where disclosure has been requested in the course of regulatory proceedings. For instance, the statements that have been kept secret so far and have not been transmitted to anyone except the lawyer and his client or to the parties and their respective counsel in the course of a joint consultation, are confidential, thus privileged. However, facts communicated by the solicitor to the client that are not subject to a confidential communication are not covered by LPP. For example, a conversation between a client and his solicitor and which the solicitor was instructed (by his client) to repeat to the other party, but not during a joint consultation, is not confidential anymore, thus not privileged (see *Conlon v Conlons Ltd.*) A solicitor cannot be compelled at the instance of a third party to disclose matters which came to his knowledge in the conduct of professional business for a client.

Furthermore, information received by a solicitor in his professional capacity from a third party and communicated by the solicitor to the client is covered by LPP. This is the doctrine supported by Justice Mervyn Davies in *Re Sarah C Getty Trust, Getty v Getty*:

> I see no ground for [...] allowing a solicitor to be questioned about what it is he may have received in a professional capacity from a third party. On the contrary, I think that to breach the blanket of privilege in the way suggested would erode to an unacceptable degree the wholesome protection that has been provided by the law for the reasons explained by Lord Brougham in *Greenhough v Gaskell* [1833]. (965)

There are some situations when the professional capacity of the lawyer is involved to a degree that justifies protection from disclosure. However, confidentiality is not a magic wand that can be used to label all documents and messages emanating from a lawyer as privileged. Justice Kay, as early as 1884, stated in *Foakes v Webb*:

> The fact that the solicitor was the person who signed a letter to the other side cannot be a confidential communication. Suppose the solicitor himself were asked that question in the witness box; he could not claim privilege and would be obliged to answer. (287)

Consequently, the protection from disclosure (the act of not testifying in the above case) stems not only from the existence of confidentiality, but also from the effective involvement of the lawyer in his professional capacity. Matters are kept secret, and privileged, not just because of the signature of the lawyer at the bottom of the document to be disclosed, but first and foremost due to the fact that the lawyer was acting in a professional capacity.

Secrecy is granted under the two forms of LPP, but the legal context differs. On the one hand, LAP protects secret, i.e. confidential communications between lawyers and their clients made for the purpose of giving or obtaining legal advice: no case is pending or envisaged at this stage. On the other hand, LP secures the secrecy of communications between lawyers, clients, and third parties made for the purposes of actual or contemplated litigation—this time, there is a case either already started by the client or in reasonable prospect. As a consequence, the scope of secrecy is as large as the range of potentially privileged documents is wide; it includes all documents either generated for the purpose of giving or getting legal advice (LPA) or stemming from actual or contemplated litigation (LP). It covers letters to or from solicitors, instructions to and opinions of counsel, working papers, drafts, and so on, provided they are all made with the dominant purpose of use in, or for obtaining evidence for, or giving or receiving legal advice in connection with the litigation. Nevertheless, secrecy has its limits since any internal correspondence with insurers within a law firm or a company such as reports for insurers, board minutes, inter-company memoranda, or reports on accidents at work are not privileged because they do not evince any sign of a professional consultation with a lawyer of any kind. At first sight, LPP seems to be in conflict with the legal requirements (transparency and disclosure) of the 1998 Civil Procedure Rules.

2. Full Disclosure

The English justice system provides that each party must be informed of the existence of all documents relevant to the case in the hands of the opposite party. Indeed, full disclosure is vital to revealing the truth in the courtroom. As a result, the current Civil Procedure Rules require that all documents, including privileged ones, be included in each party's list of disclosed documents. On the website of the Ministry of Justice, one may download the official guidelines regarding the disclosure and inspection of documents set out in Part 31 of the CPR. Pursuant to those rules, disclosure does not mean that one party will entirely unveil the contents of the documents of the case. It is just a form of assertion of the current or former existence of these documents. Rule 31.2 states that "A party discloses a document by stating that the document exists or has existed". The parties to a case are aware of the existence of such documents, but their actual content may be kept secret.

> Secrets may be perfectly known, and thereby protected, in full transparency. The transparency over the secret's existence is precisely of way of ensuring the respect of its content. (Ferrier 2000, 115) (my translation)

Secrecy works as a restriction of transparency: disclosed documents can be inspected unless protected by LPP.

First of all, each party prepares and transmits a list of specific documents to all other parties using the relevant practice form (N265), called "list of documents: standard disclosure". The nature of these documents is quite precise: they are "documents of whose existence the party is aware that fall within Rule 31.6" (Practice Direction 31A, 1)

> Standard disclosure requires a party to disclose only–
> (a) the documents on which he relies; and
> (b) the documents which–
> (i) adversely affect his own case;
> (ii) adversely affect another party's case; or
> (iii) support another party's case; and
> (c) the documents which he is required to disclose by a relevant practice direction [Rule 31.6]

Secondly, in the same form N265, on the last page, the disclosing party must clearly list and number the documents under his control which he objects to being inspected pursuant to Rule 31.19. He must also specify his justifications for withholding the inspection. Whenever a document has been disclosed in the required list, the disclosing party has two options, either letting the other party inspect those documents or invoking the right (or duty) to withhold the inspection under the procedure set out in Rule 31.19. To invoke LPP, the disclosing party must include a written statement in the disclosure statement (form N265), indicating "the document, or part of a document, to which the claim relates" (Practice Direction 31A, 4.6, 2) as well as "the grounds on which he claims that right or duty. (Practice Direction 31A, 4.5(2), 2) Protection from disclosure is granted to any party wishing not to disclose a document "without notice", that is to say that no application to the court is actually required. (Practice Direction 31A, 6.1, 3)

In rule 31.19.(3), an important distinction is drawn between a person who wishes to claim that he has a right to withhold inspection—the party itself—and the person who wishes to claim that he has a duty to withhold inspection—the lawyer. The principle of LPP is a right attached to the client, not the lawyer as recalled by Lord Taylor in R v. Derby:

> [...] this case is thus clear authority for the rule that the privilege is that of the client, which he alone can waive, and that the court will not permit, let alone order, the attorney to reveal the

confidential communications which have passed between him and his former client. (para 48)

In England and Wales, solicitors must observe standards and requirements set out in a special book, called the Solicitors' Regulation Handbook (SRA). Among these rules, one provides that a lawyer has to "keep the affairs of clients confidential unless disclosure is required or permitted by law or the *client* consents" (SRA Handbook, O(4.1).). Only the client may put an end to the secrecy by waiving his right to withhold inspection of confidential and privileged documents.

Consequently, once a party has made a claim to withhold inspection, LPP removes any obligation imposed on the disclosing party to allow inspection. Under Rule 31.3, "[...] A party to whom a document has been disclosed has a right to inspect that document except where [...] the party disclosing the document has a right or a duty to withhold inspection of it." Once a claim of confidentiality has been made, the party who wants to inspect the disclosed documents may file an application to challenge such a claim pursuant to Rule 31.19 (5). Finally, there is a procedure, set out in Rules 31.19 (1) and (6) that "enables a party to apply for an order permitting disclosure of the existence of a document to be withheld" i.e. affirmed by the court. This leads to the conflicting situation where a party knows the existence of documents in the hands of the other party, and yet has no access to their privileged contents.

Two main issues arise from the intrusion of secrecy within an allegedly transparent adversarial system. First of all, by preventing the communications between a client and his counsel from being disclosed in a court of law, LPP can deny the party access to relevant documents; it jeopardizes the fairness of the proceedings and the general public interest that "requires that in the interests of a fair trial litigation should be conducted on the footing that all relevant documentary evidence is available" (*Grant v. Downs* (1976) 135 C.LR., 674, 685, Stephen, Mason and Murphy JJ., cited in *R v. Derby* para 73). The existence of this privilege which is deeply anchored in English law seems to be detrimental to the general fairness advocated at the core of the justice system. Secondly, confidentiality is a central figure of lawyers' ethics. It is part and parcel of a code (and right) of silence they have to abide by as legal advisers. It prohibits them to disclose any information regarding their clients' affairs. At the same time, LPP enables them to shroud in secret activities carried out in their capacity as legal counsel, thus preventing any full and fair assessment of the ethical dimension of their performance. As said earlier, LPP entitles a party to a dispute not to disclose information no matter how relevant it is to the issue to be determined by a court. Even though players are encouraged to play with their cards on the table, secrecy is also clearly embedded in the rules of the game under specific requirements.

Requirements to Acknowledge LAP

For the purpose of clarity, this part of the paper focuses on the first category of LPP, legal advice privilege for which Lord Carswell gave a broad definition in *Three Rivers No 6*:

> [...] all communications between a solicitor and his client relating to a transaction in which the solicitor has been instructed for the purpose of obtaining legal advice will be privileged, notwithstanding that they do not contain advice on matters of law or construction, provided that they are directly related to the performance by the solicitor of his professional duty as legal adviser of his client. (para 111)

English case law has established a two-fold test to determine the conditions under which someone is entitled to invoke LAP. Two important cases set out the criteria of the test to determine the nature and the context of the communications.

Firstly, in *Balabel v Air India*, Lord Justice Taylor ruled in favor of a broad construction of the purposes of legal advice. The act of providing legal advice cannot be narrowly interpreted as simply explaining the law to a client:

> [...] the purpose and scope of the privilege is still to enable legal advice to be sought and given in confidence. [...] therefore, the test is whether the communication or other document was made confidentially for the purposes of legal advice. Those purposes have to be construed broadly. [...] Moreover, legal advice is not confined to telling the client the law; it must include advice as to what should prudently and sensibly be done in the relevant legal context. (330)

Accordingly, were the rule construed as applying only to communications specifically seeking or conveying advice, it would be too narrow, thus depriving clients of legal privilege in most situations. Lord Justice Taylor goes on to explain:

> Once solicitors are embarked on a [...] transaction they are employed to ensure that the client steers clear of legal difficulties, and communications passing in the handling of that transaction are privileged (if their aim is the obtaining of appropriate legal advice) since the whole handling is experience and legal skill in action and a document uttered during the transaction does not have to incorporate a specific piece of legal advice to obtain that privilege. (*Ibid.*, 332)

Secondly, in *Three Rivers No 6*, Lord Scott proposed a test to determine the existence of a "relevant legal context" for the communication:

> In cases of doubt the judge [...] should ask whether the advice related to the rights, liabilities, obligations or remedies of the client, either under private law or under public law. If it does not, then, in my opinion, legal advice privilege would not apply. (para 38)

In 1992, the government commissioned an independent inquiry headed by Lord Bingham to consider whether the supervision of the collapsed Bank of Credit and Commerce International (BCCI) was adequate and whether action taken by the UK authorities was timely. The Bank of England was the focus of the inquiry. It set up an in-house team of three employees, called the BIU (Bingham Inquiry Unit) whose role was to deal with requests of information from the Bingham inquiry. The Bank also instructed several solicitors and counsel. A group of BCCI's creditors issued proceedings against the Bank of England for failing to regulate the BCCI properly. They required the Bank to disclose internal Bank material created during the Bingham Inquiry into the BCCI collapse and communicated to the BIU or the instructed solicitors. The Bank claimed legal advice privilege for the internal Bank documents and argued that these were created for the dominant purpose of obtaining legal advice.

In *Three Rivers (No 5)*, the Court of Appeal initially decided that employees of the Bank were third parties and that all documents they prepared could not be covered by legal advice privilege. This was a departure from *Balabel* in so far as it narrowly construed the concept of a "client" which now comprises only the people tasked with liaising directly with lawyers; employees of a company are no longer automatically assumed to act as agents for the client. The term "lawyer" includes both in-house counsel and external lawyers. However, in *Three Rivers (No 6)*, the House of Lords reaffirmed *Balabel* while overturning the Court of Appeal. They ruled that communications between the BIU and the Bank's external lawyers were privileged only if they were made for the purpose of the giving or receiving of "legal advice", i.e. advice on the party's legal rights and obligations. They held that the Court of Appeal's view of "legal advice" was too narrow; they overruled *No 5* by reaffirming the existence of LAP. The Law Lords asserted that people should be able to consult their lawyers in confidence to achieve orderly arrangement of their affairs, irrespective of the potential for litigation. Provided a lawyer has been instructed to act in a "relevant legal context", then any confidential communication between client and lawyer related to the performance of the lawyer's duties should be protected, not just those communications containing advice on the law.

As a consequence, LAP applies only to communications between the client and members of the legal professional (solicitors and barristers) as well as legally qualified in-house lawyers acting as their capacity as such. This can also be a compliance officer if and only he has formal legal qualifications and regularly gives advice of a legal nature Thus, in order to invoke LAP, the party must prove that the communications in question were made with a professional legal adviser and with the sole or dominant purpose of giving or obtaining legal advice. Moreover, judges have to determine whether the communications in question fall within the policy underlying the justification for LAP in English case law.

Having presented the conditions to meet so as to invoke privilege, it is now relevant to return to the question raised in the introduction to this paper: how can one account for such a deeply anchored principle of secrecy between client and lawyer knowing that it has to function within the framework of a procedure based on disclosure?

Justifications of LPP

What legitimizes such a form of secrecy within a transparent system? One may first look at the rules implemented to make the justice system work. Rule 31.19 previously quoted provides that an application or a claim for withholding documents must be grounded on the fact that "disclosure would damage the public interest." Once again, it seems necessary to refer to English case law in order to interpret the expression "public interest".

> But it is out of regard to the interests of justice [...] and the administration of justice, which cannot go on, in the practice of the Courts. (*Greenough* 103)

> The relation between the client and his professional legal adviser is a confidential relation of such a nature that to my mind the maintenance of the privilege with regard to it is essential to the interests of justice and the well-being of society. (*Southwark and Vauxhall Water Co.* v. *Quick* (1877) cited in *R. v. Derby* para 53)

> The client must be sure that what he tells his lawyer in confidence will never be revealed without his consent. Legal professional privilege is thus much more than an ordinary rule of evidence, limited in its application to the facts of a particular case. It is a fundamental condition on which the administration of justice as a whole rests.[...] But in the overall interests of the administration of justice it is better that the principle should be preserved intact. (*R. v. Derby*, paras 60 and 69)

> The rationale of this head of privilege [...] is that it promotes the public interest because it assists and enhances the administration of justice by facilitating the representation of clients by advisers, the law being a complex and complicated discipline. (*Grant v. Downs* (1976) cited in *R. v. Derby* para 73)

The meaning of "public interest" within the legal context of professional privilege can be deduced from the above quotations. Firstly, the public interest means better access to justice, a more satisfactory and efficient administration of justice. Law being difficult, people need the legal skills of professionals to guide them in the tangle of technicalities. One of the main missions carried out by a lawyer is to facilitate the access and understanding of law since it is often not easy for the layman to grasp its meaning. With laws becoming ever more numerous, the average citizen needs to be kept informed by law practitioners even outside any pending litigation. Lord Hoffmann put forward this argument in *R (Morgan Grenfell Ltd) v Special Commissioner of Income Tax.* He referred to LPP as "a fundamental human right long established in the common law [...] a necessary corollary of the right of any person to obtain skilled advice about the law" (para 7). By securing the secrecy of any communication between client and lawyer, English legal procedure provides an easier access to justice insofar as people are not afraid of contacting a legal professional for their assistance.

Unless LPP is an absolute protection, anyone can be deprived of legal aid and professional advice "upon the subject of his rights and his liabilities, with no reference to any particular litigation" (*Greenough* 103). Consequently, the entire administration of justice without at its core LPP would be jeopardized leaving people "deprived of all professional assistance" who "would not venture to consult any skillful person, or would only dare to tell his counsellor half his case" [*ibid*]. To conclude, the first underlying purpose of privilege is to enable anyone to have access to a lawyer's professional skills and judgment as illustrated in the quotation below:

> It is common ground that the basic principle justifying legal professional privilege arises from the public interest requiring full and frank exchange of confidence between solicitor and client to enable the latter to receive necessary legal advice. (*Balabel* 327)

LPP is a key principle for the administration of justice. It is also the cornerstone of a relationship of trust between clients and lawyers. Indeed, it is described as "a species of confidence" (Thanki 2006, 1). In *Three Rivers No 6*, Lord Scott of Foscote stated that "legal advice privilege arises out of a relationship of confidence between lawyer and client" (para 24). Similarly, in *Balabel*, Lord Taylor of Gosforth CJ said the following:

> The principle which runs through all these cases ... is that a man must be able to consult his lawyer in confidence, since otherwise he might hold back half the truth. The client must be sure that what he tells his lawyer in confidence will never be revealed without his consent. (507)

Secrecy between a client and his lawyer is a necessary requirement, a blessing in disguise, for confidence's sake.

Privilege has a sound basis in common sense. It exists for the purpose of ensuring that there shall be complete and unqualified confidence in the mind of a client when he goes to his solicitor, or when he goes to his counsel, that which he there divulges will never be disclosed to anybody else. It is only if the client feels safe in making a clean breast of his troubles to his advisers that litigation and the business of the law can be carried on satisfactorily [...] There is an abundance of authority in support of the proposition that once legal professional privilege attaches to a document [...] that privilege attaches for all time and in all circumstances (*Hobbs v. Hobbs* [1960] Justice Stevenson, 116–117, cited in *R v. Derby*, para 56). LPP is the vital "basis of the confidence" (*R v. Derby* para 69) between a lawyer and a (potential) client. Without LPP, such confidence would be "undermined or destroyed" (*ibid.*) or "necessarily lost" (*Balabel* 508). The necessity of secrecy to build and secure trust between clients and lawyers is a recurrent rationale supported by English judges.

> [...] communications between a party and his professional advisers, with a view to legal proceedings, should be unfettered; and they should not be restrained by any apprehension of such communications being afterwards divulged and made use of to his prejudice. [...] The necessary confidence will be destroyed if it be known that the communication can be revealed at any time. (*Holmes v. Baddeley* [1844] 1 Ph., Lord Lyndhurst L.C., 480–481, cited in *R. v. Derby*, para 51)

> [...] a lawyer must be able to give his client an absolute and unqualified assurance that whatever the client tells him in confidence will never be disclosed without his consent. (*B v Auckland District Law Society*, 757)

LPP aims at "unrestricted and unbounded confidence" (*R v. Derby* para 52), that is to say full disclosure. Instead of locking up litigants in a world of lies and deceit, LPP helps persuade clients who need the assistance of a lawyer to "make a clean breast of it to the gentleman whom he consults with a view to the prosecution of his claim, or substantiating his defence against the claim of others" (*Anderson v. Bank of British Columbia* (1876) 2 Ch, 649, cited in *R. v. Derby*, para 52), not to "hold back half the truth" (*R v. Derby*, para 58) leading them to a "full and frank disclosure of the relevant circumstances to the solicitor" (*Grant v. Downs* cited in *R v. Derby*, para 73).

> Rightly or wrongly, the provisions often shaped by past relationships, indiscretions, experiences, impressions and mistakes, as well as by jealousies, slights, animosities and affections, which the testator would not to have revealed but which he must nev-

ertheless explain if the solicitor is to carry out his wishes. (*Three Rivers* 2004, para 55)

Consequently, an absence of secrecy in the first place would be a deterrent from telling the whole truth to one's lawyer, leading to more harm and misery if confidential communications were to be unveiled. People can be fairly represented and defended only if they trust their counsel and do not fear that any of what has been confined to their legal adviser will be revealed. Transparency is, thus, a necessity in order to restore, if not establish, a relation of trust indispensable to the good working of social rules (Ferrier 2000, 122) (my translation). It is a key to a good understanding of the law. Counter-intuitively, secrecy and trust are intertwined, the former being a necessary requirement to the very existence of the latter. It is vital for any client to trust their lawyer without fearing any prejudice to the potential or ongoing case. Better legal advice is guaranteed thanks to LPP. In fact, if no secrecy is protected between a lawyer and another party, it may then lead to deception. Transparency is sometimes only preserved through secrecy and confidentiality.

The correlation between the quality of the legal services provided by lawyers and the confidentiality of their communications is repeatedly highlighted in English case law.

> If the advice given by lawyers is to be sound, their clients must make them aware of all the relevant circumstances of the problem. [...] And there is little or no chance of the client taking the right or sensible course if the lawyer's advice is inaccurate or unsound because the lawyer has been given an incomplete or inaccurate picture of the client's position. (*Three Rivers* paras 54 and 61)

> Such advice cannot be effectively obtained unless the client is able to put all the facts before the adviser without fear that they may afterwards be disclosed and used to his prejudice. (*R v Special Commissioner* 607)

If there is no guarantee that every word or note transmitted between a client and his lawyer is protected from disclosure, the freedom of legal communication will be impaired, preventing any person from confiding in their counsel. Among the policy justifications of LPP lies the idea of sound legal advice: a lawyer will be more efficient, providing more accurate and well-reasoned legal advice when better informed. He is all the more well-in-formed when his client feels safe and willing to communicate matters he might have been tempted to omit. To provide someone, and in particular a client, with the best possible defence, the lawyer requires full disclosure on the part of his client. But for the protection of strict confidentiality, the client might be inhibited to disclose everything to his counsel. This is the reason why LPP is applied to legal advisers, barristers and solicitors in pri-vate practice, salaried (in-house) legal advisers employed by government departments or commercial companies, as well as foreign lawyers:

> There is nothing [in the previous case law concerning privilege] to suggest that [the judges] intended to limit the rule to legal advisers whose names appear on the role of Solicitors of the Su-preme Court or who are members of the English Bar. The basis of the privilege is just as apt to cover foreign legal advisers as En-glish lawyers, provided only that the relationship of lawyer and client subsists between them. (Justice Ormrod in *Re Duncan, Garfield v Fay* [1968], 311)

However, LPP does not cover communications between a person and a nonlegally qualified adviser (*New Victoria Hospital v Ryan* [1993] ICR 201, EAT) or members of other professions (*Slade v Tucker* [1880] 14 Ch. D 824). By affording a distinct, invaluable right to have communica-tions protected from compelled disclosure to any third party, LPP helps clients feel secure to talk to their legal counsel with no second thoughts or half-truths.

3. LIMITS ON SECRECY?

To some, LPP may appear as an exception to the general principle of full disclosure vital to the unveiling of the truth in the courtroom insofar as it grants exceptional and extensive protection from otherwise compulso-ry disclosure to all privileged communications. One may think that LPP should be decided on a "balancing exercise", on a case-by-case assessment of the facts; whenever there is a reason for non-disclosure (LPP), it may be outweighed by other considerations. Judges should weigh the public inter-est of keeping client–lawyer information confidential (secrecy) on the one hand and the necessary transparency of legal proceedings to secure a fair trial on the other hand. This is what happened in *R v. Derby*. In this case, under section 97 of the Magistrates' Courts Act 1980 the appellant was required to produce documents by a witness summons granted by the Derby Stipendiary Magistrate, in the course of committal proceedings against the appellant's stepfather. The latter was accused of the murder of a 16-year-old girl more than 25 years previously. The judge who granted the summons initially ruled that the necessity to have the appellant testify in court prevailed over the confidentiality of what this person told his counsel during criminal proceedings. He considered the possibility to limit LPP by weighing competing public interests against each other.

There is an "interaction between two aspects of the public interest in the administration of justice" as identified by Lord Nicholls of Birkenhead in *R v Derby*:

> That is one aspect of the public interest. It takes the form of according to the client a right, or privilege as it is unhelpfully called, to withhold disclosure of the contents of client–lawyer communications. In the ordinary course the client has an interest in asserting this right, in so far as disclosure would or might prejudice him. [...] The other aspect of the public interest is that all relevant material should be available to courts when deciding cases. Courts should not have to reach decisions in ignorance of the contents of documents or other material which, if disclosed, might well affect the outcome." (paras 72 and 73)

This quotation clearly highlights the existing link between the necessary access to sound legal advice, the presence of uninhibited communication between clients and lawyers, and the fact that to be efficient, the administration of justice should be left in ignorance of material relevant to the case (actual or potential). In this situation, LPP sounds problematic; by restricting "the power of the court to compel the production of what would otherwise be relevant evidence" (*Three Rivers* para 61), by preventing client–lawyer communications from being disclosed in a court of law, the privilege either denies one party access to documents that may prove relevant to the case, or restricts the requested access to these materials and "may impede the proper administration of justice in the individual case" (*ibid.*). Thus, it jeopardizes the fairness of the procedure that should put both parties on an equal footing.

However, if a balance between the right to transparency—to be able to inspect the other party's documents—and the right to secrecy—of the disclosing party who invokes LPP as a protection from that inspection—has to be struck, how can it be achieved? On what grounds or objective legal criteria? This tricky question was answered by judges who rejected the idea of a "balancing exercise". They argued that LPP was an absolute rule of immunity (*Three Rivers* para 25), so legitimate that it needed full protection and suffered no exception whatsoever. According to Lord Taylor of Gosforth and Lord Lloyd of Berwick in *R v. Derby* (paras 34 and 67), there should be no balancing exercise because LPP is "the predominant public interest" that must be upheld unless waived:

> In exercising this discretion the court would be faced with an essentially impossible task. One man's meat is another man's poison (explanation: disclosure may beneficial to one party but detrimental to another) [...] This highlights the impossibility of the exercise. [...] In the absence of principled answers to these and similar questions, and I can see none, there is no escaping the conclusion that the prospect of a judicial balancing exercise in this field is illusory, a veritable will-o'-the-wisp. That in itself is a sufficient reason for not departing from the established law. (*R. v. Derby*, paras 78 and 79)

Once established, LPP cannot be weighed against any countervailing public interest factor as stated in *R v. Derby*: "once privileged, always privileged" (para 41). Lord Taylor of Gosforth even reminded the court that "no exception should be allowed to the absolute nature of legal professional privilege, once established" (*ibid.*, para 65). As argued by Thanki, this privilege is now a substantive right of considerable importance, and as such cannot be lightly overridden (1.06).

There are two situations where a limit is put on LPP. The first one deals with the right of the client to waive his privilege by disclosing (or allowing his solicitor to disclose) confidential communications. The veil of secrecy is then lifted on the client's sole initiative. English law provides the principle of selective waiver: a party may choose to disclose one or several documents to a third party for a limited purpose while keeping the very confidentiality of this same legally privileged document as long as it has not entered the public domain. Secondly, the scope of LPP should be limited to the instance in which the lawyer acts as a professional legal adviser. As soon as his part becomes one of "a public man" (*Greenough*, 109), for example by becoming a party to a fraud or acting for himself and not for his client, LPP no longer applies. Any communication between a client suspected of fraud and his solicitor even if the latter is unaware of the illegal business, is not privileged and should be disclosed as criminal or fraudulent activities that are "injurious to the interest of justice" (*R v Cox and Railton*, 167) because a "communication in furtherance of a criminal purpose does not come into "the ordinary scope of professional employment" (*ibid.*). Two partners, Mr. Cox and Mr. Railton, were tried and convicted on a charge of conspiring to defraud a judgment creditor, Mr. Munster, of the fruits of his execution. At the trial, a solicitor, Mr. Goodman, was called by the prosecution to testify that after Mr. Munster had obtained his judgment, Mr. Cox and Mr. Railton consulted him as to how they might defeat that judgment. The admissibility of that evidence was questioned on the grounds that the communications were between client and solicitor, thus privileged.

Secrecy is a sacrosanct principle only preserved between lawyer and client if it is based on the legal nature of the intervention of the legal adviser. Acting as a co-conspirator, as "the party acting, rather than the attorney entrusted, the principal rather than the agent" (*Greenough*, 109), he will no longer be able to use legal professional privilege as a shield to conceal his actions. He will be bound to disclose all relevant matters. Thus, the degree of secrecy depends on the professional nature of the bond between lawyer and client, on the status of the legal adviser who should not be involved personally, but strictly professionally. What this analysis has revealed is that secrecy is actually close to neutrality, applied for the sole purpose of avoiding deceit, co-conspiracy, or complicity. But for the professional dimension of the lawyer-client relation, all communications between the two would not be recognized as privileged. Cases as early as *Greenough* have clearly established that there is no protection from disclosure if the nature of the communication is not professional, but just casual (like addressing a friend) or "in the usual course of business" (*Greenough*, 115). So, if someone says something or writes something or communicates in any way to someone not as a professional, if some papers or documents are "confided to someone not professionally" (*Greenough*, 106) or if a lawyer becomes acquainted with some information not in his professional capacity, then legal privilege does not stand and cannot be argued to refuse to disclose relevant documents.

Furthermore, should any exception to the rule of privilege be tolerated, it would have to be explicitly supported by primary legislation: "An intention to override such rights may be expressly stated or appear by necessary implication" (R *(Morgan Grenfell Ltd) v Special Commissioner of Income Tax*, para 8). Indeed, LPP may only be overridden expressly by statute, but the curtailment of privilege can only be to the extent "reasonably necessary" to meet the ends which justify the curtailment.[1] One can quote a rare example of LPP being overridden by statute with the Regulation of Investigatory Powers Act 2000, a piece of legislation construed as authorizing communications between persons in custody and their legal advisers to be under covert surveillance. The court held that this statute did by implication override legal professional privilege in *McE v Prison Service of Northern Ireland*.

CONCLUSION

Secrecy within a relevant legal context has now been recognized as "a fundamental human right protected by the European Convention for the Protection of Human Rights and Fundamental Freedoms" (R v. Derby para 61). In Campbell v United Kingdom, the court ruled that the routine opening of correspondence flowing between a secure category prisoner and his solicitor violated the prisoner's Article 8 rights. In 1983, in AM&S v Commission of the European communities, a case about a company investigated for a suspected breach of Article 81 or 82 EC, the European Court established the principle that Regulation 17 (now replaced by Regulation 1/2003) must be interpreted as protecting the confidentiality of written communications between lawyer and client if two conditions are met: the communications have to be made for the purpose and in the interests of the client's right of defence and the communications emanate from independent lawyers established within the EU. Nowadays, lawyers are required to respect a duty of confidentiality: they have to live by a code of silence which prohibits disclosure of information concerning their clients' affairs. English law, through its adversarial procedure, has technically reconciled transparency and secrecy. Secrecy is at the service of transparency which, in its turn, is a vital requirement for legal professional privilege.

---

1   R v. *Secretary of State for the Home Department*, paras 5 and 31.

BIBLIOGRAPHY

Primary sources

Form N265. "List of documents: standard disclosure." March 2013. <http://hmctscourtfinder.justice.gov.uk/courtfinder/forms/n265-eng.pdf>.

Practice direction 31a–Disclosure and Inspection. March 2013. <http://www.justice.gov.uk/pre-trash-archive/civ-proc-rules-old/_old/pd_part31a>.

Rules of Civil Procedure, Part 31. March 2013. <http://www.justice.gov.uk/courts/procedure-rules/civil/rules/part31>.

Solicitors' Regulation Handbook (SRA). March 2013. <http://www.sra.org.uk/solicitors/handbook/pdfcentre.page>.

Cases

Greenough v Gaskell [1833] 39 E.R. 618.

Slade v Tucker [1880] 14 Ch. D 824.

Foakes v Webb [1884] UKHL 1.

R v Cox and Railton [1884] 14 QBD 153.

Conlon v Conlons Ltd [1952] 2 All ER 462, CA.

Re Duncan, Garfield v Fay [1968] P 306.

AM&S v Commission of the European communities case 155/179 [1983] QB 878.

Re Sarah C Getty Trust, Getty v Getty [1985] QB 956.

Balabel and Another v. Air India, Court of Appeal [1988] Ch. 317.

Campbell v United Kingdom [1992] 15 EHRR 137.

New Victoria Hospital v Ryan [1993] ICR 201, EAT.

R v Derby Magistrates' Court, ex p B [1996] AC 487.

R v. Secretary of State for the Home Department, ex p Daly [2001] 2 AC 532.

B v Auckland District Law Society [2003] 2 AC 736.

R (Morgan Grenfell Ltd) v Special Commissioner of Income Tax [2003] 1 AC 563.

Three Rivers District Council v Bank of England (No 5) [2003] EWCA Civ 474.

Three Rivers District Council v Bank of England (No 6) [2004] UKHL 48.

Secondary sources

Ferrier, D. 2000. "Secret et transparence." In *Secret et justice, le secret entre éthique et technique?*, eds. J. P. Royer and B. Durand. Lille: L'espace juridique, 109–134.

Dumaine, L. 2000. "Le secret professionnel de l'avocat au XXème siècle." In *Secret et justice, le secret entre éthique et technique?*, eds. J. P. Royer and B. Durand. Lille: L'espace juridique, 277–289.

Luban, D. 1998. *Lawyers and Justice: An Ethical Study*. Princeton University Press.

Slapper, G., and D. Kelly. 2010. *English Law*. Routledge-Cavendish.

Thanki, B. 2006. *The Law of Privilege*. Oxford: Oxford University Press.

www.ingramcontent.com/pod-product-compliance
Lightning Source LLC
Chambersburg PA
CBHW071236290326
41931CB00038B/3106